WAVERLY PUBLIC LIBRARY

3 6696 42330 5880

RENÉE WENDINGER

LAST TRAIN HOME

*An abridged historical fiction
regarding the largest mass
migration of children known
as the orphan trains.*

Waverly Public Library
1500 West Bremer Ave.
Waverly, IA 50677

D1605644

514

This book is a work of historical fiction.
It blends characters, adventures, and dates into
a demographic spectrum for readers of all ages.

LAST TRAIN HOME. Copyright © 2014 by Renée Wendinger.
All rights reserved. Printed in the United States of America.
No part of this book may be reproduced in any form, by photocopying
or by any electronic or mechanical means, including information storage
or retrieval systems, without permission in writing from the copyright
author or publisher.

This material has been written and published for educational purposes. The
author and the publisher shall have neither liability nor responsibility to any
person or entity with respect to any loss, damage, or injury caused or alleged
to be caused directly or indirectly by the information contained in this book.

Published by: Legendary Publications, Minnesota

ISBN: 978-0-9913603-0-7
Library of Congress Control Number: 2013958352
First Edition

Front Cover: Swindon Train Silhouette.

Images authorized by owner, John Beresford of Great Britain.

ACKNOWLEDGMENTS

Thank you, mom (Sophia), for sharing your life story with your children through the years. You have done a beautiful job of raising each of your five children, and we are the lucky ones to have you for our mother. Thank you, dad (Charles Hillesheim), for "sweeping mom off her feet."

As of this writing, Sophia is ninety-eight years old and one of the few survivors of the orphan train. She truly lived a Cinderella story.

I would like to extend immense gratitude to Clarice, Kenny, Sam, John, William, and Lorraine Arsers and their families for sharing the life story of their grandfather, John Arsers. Had it not been for John's journalistic insight, and Julia's letters, much history would have been lost. The stories of John and Sophia are profound examples of a quarter of a million children who rode the orphan trains throughout America from the East Coast. They rose above challenging circumstances to live positive and productive lives. I am in awe of their strength to triumph over adversity.

I would like to thank Mount Holyoke College, Archives and Special Collections, South Hadley, Massachusetts, for the Harriet M. (North) Dowd Papers where complete Dowd and North family letters are archived. I would like to extend grateful appreciation to Mary Noble, a relative of Orrin Mildrum, for letter interpretations and extractions of family history, and photographs.

Comparably, I'd like to express an extensive thank you to *The New York Children's Aid Society*, the *New York Foundling*, the *New York Historical Society*, and the *New York Times*, for examination of conserved documents.

Thank you to the families of William and Anne Ochs for promises and assurances of love, trust, and encouragement given to my mother, Sophia.

Significant appreciation to John Shontz, historian for the Milwaukee Road and Upper Musselshell Historical Society, Harlowton, Montana, and 'all the railroad guys' of the New York Central, for mapping out the train journeys of Sophia and Johnny. Additionally to Anita Shontz for getting the wheels turning, and Alisa Aetzel and the expert map designers at Morrison-Mariele, Inc. Montana, for the visual elements of Sophia's train journey reminiscent of the hundreds of thousands of children that traveled over America's rails by orphan trains.

Thank you, Patricia, Charlene, Johnora, and Stephen, my extraordinary siblings, for your dependable and supportive encouragement in writing this story. Your motivation has pulled me through once again to realize this book.

Gratitude to God for lovingly awarding my life with three beautiful children, Lee, Jennifer, and Terry, and their spouses. Likewise, to my grandchildren, Jaydon, Alison, Lily, Landon, Karly, and Kenlee. You will forever hold my heart in your hands.

And to my husband, Lonnie—for your endless patience when it was most required.

For my mother Sophia,
with all my love

Half to forget the wandering and the pain,
Half to remember days that have gone by,
And dream and dream that I am home again!

James Elroy Flecker
poet, novelist, and playwright

INTRODUCTION

The Orphan Trains

During the nineteenth and early twentieth centuries, the streets of New York were overrun with tens of thousands of penniless orphans. To address this problem, the New York Children's Aid Society was established by Charles Loring Brace, and the New York Foundling Hospital soon came into being under the able guidance of Sister Irene Fitzgibbon. From 1854 to 1929, these two institutions, along with supplementary East Coast orphanages, transported over 250,000 children across America by train to find families and homes. The orphan trains, as they were known, provided the means for a great migration from hopelessness to opportunity rescuing the children of America's immigrant poor from neglect and cruelty on the streets of New York.

New York City was then the leading entry point for immigrants into the United States. Massive numbers were crammed into overcrowded housing in the city, especially in the Lower East Side, the port of entry for the destitute. This soon brought about poverty, disease, and corruption. Many found hardships equal those they thought they had left behind, and their sufferings soon became their children's.

Thirty-four thousand vagrant children lived on the streets of New York City in the mid-1850. Endless numbers of children had been found on doorsteps or in ash barrels, gutters, vacant lots, and other out-of-the-way places. Many were dead or dying from exposure and hunger before Charles Loring Brace, a minister turned social worker, devised an emigration plan, the orphan trains, to send children away from the over-populated city streets. He believed he could find family homes for these waifs in the West, a place that held up the promise of a wholesome atmosphere in which to raise children. Yet he struggled with the dilemma of what to do with all these children. He once acknowledged that "when a child of the streets stands before you in rags, with a tear-stained face, you cannot easily forget him. And yet, you are perplexed what to do. The human soul is difficult to interfere with. You hesitate how far you should go."

Thousands of children were shipped out of New York City on trains bound for America's heartland and beyond during the 1800s and early 1900s. The trains were the next leg of the journey for countless children of immigrant parents. Many of these children were not orphans. Most had no less than one living parent. They were children whose guardians could not care for them beyond their circumstances or whose parents had anticipated their offspring would find better lives than the ones they could provide. Other children, typically adolescents without known guardians, were seeking adventure in the West. They came west by means of lodging houses, or from industrial schools recruited by the Society's agents, whereas others were transferred to the care of the Children's Aid from the streets or from orphanages, almshouses, and correctional facilities.

Traveling from town to town, these children were displayed on train station platforms and in town halls where prospective parents could choose a child who looked strong enough for hard work or endearing enough to provide female companionship for a lonely farm wife. Overall, these children went to forty-seven states and were taken to sod houses and cabins, to large and small farms, and to shopkeeper's homes in towns. They became sons and daughters or indentured servants and were sometimes indigent, sometimes prosperous.

The New York Foundling Hospital, operated by Sister Irene Fitzgibbon and the Sisters of Charity, following the order of Saint Elizabeth Ann Seton, were child savers too, but they reserved safekeeping to infants and young children. Crime seemed to follow poverty, and the most monstrous crime of all was infanticide. The sisters began sending Baby Trains or Baby Specials west throughout a course of sixty years, beginning in 1869. The sisters commissioned prospective parents to apply for and order a child in advance through parish priests, merely by arranging for an unseen child by affirmation of hair and eye color, age, and gender.

In the course of seventy-five years, the orphan trains traveled west transporting its precious cargo until legislature passed laws for better social conditions and child welfare. Each program was controversial, even for those for whom the journey ultimately was a triumph. Others found the transition from one life to another a mêlée of circumstances.

John Arsers, sent west from the New York Children's Aid Society and Sophia Kaminsky from the New York Foundling Hospital, were two of the many children of the train. Their life stories tell the personal side of an epoch in history blending characters, adventures, and dates into émigrés of distinction.

I

JOHNNY'S STORY

*"I was born in Italy and went by the male
French name Jean [John.] My name in
Italy and France was Jean Assero and
Jean Assers (pronounced Zhahn Ashers)."*

–Johnny

Johnny scarcely remembered attending his mother's funeral in northern Italy. The young Italian boy was about the age of three or four. The only detail existing in his young mind was that his Mama was gone. Sometime later, his father remarried selling Johnny's birthright to a mess of pottage. The lad endured daily thrashings dished out by his callous step-mother, often sending him skulking for cover.

It is not known exactly when, but Johnny was taken from his home while in Italy, and then kept in someone else's house. He was not allowed to open the door or go outside without someone by his side. Soon after, these unfamiliar people tied him to a burro, and in the night they all started across the mountains. Traveling for several days and nights they finally came to an unidentified village. After that, Johnny recalls staying with a man and a woman for a period of time, and once the lady of the house taking him to a church, where she received strange looks from onlookers. She immediately picked him up and quickly ran home with him after the sermon. Johnny had no idea why, but again he became hidden from the world, and wasn't allowed outside. Then one day, a man arrived at this house, took Johnny away, and placed him on a very large boat with giant sails.

Johnny was on the boat for an extensive amount of time, and after a great deal of traveling he arrived in Paris, France in 1869-1870. There he was met by a man and woman. The man considering himself the "head of the family," took him to their hovel. Unknowingly, five-year-old Johnny was now a prisoner of the Padrone System.

> *"We were in Paris at least a year or two, playing*
> *and begging. We had two harps, violin and viola.*
> *I played the triangle besides. I have scars on my body*
> *and my wrists where I was tied up and whipped for not*
> *bringing home enough money at night. I lived on rye*
> *bread, and sometimes a small piece of cheese, or whatever*
> *I could pick up on the streets. Quite often we would*
> *get separated from each other, and I would sleep just*
> *any place, or the police would pick me up, and the next*
> *morning the "father of the family" would come and get*
> *me, and that always meant a good whipping."*

–Johnny

The padrone was an indentured labor system that preyed upon Italian immigrants to the United States. Thousands of Italians, young and old alike found themselves prisoners of the padrone [from the Italian *padroni* for "patrons" or "bosses.] The *padroni* would be one of their own, and was the original 'Don.' In practice, many *padroni* acted more like slave holders than managers controlling the wages, contracts, and food supply under his authority, and could keep workers on the job for weeks or months beyond their contracts.

"In Paris, the headquarters of the infamous business, the children are handed over to a bureau, which sends them to all civilized countries. In 1867, the number of *padroni* in Paris reports 1,544. In 1868 and 1869, they were found to be 698 and 431 respectively, owing to the business having been largely transferred to London and New York. This unnatural trade is spoken of as kidnapping. For the Kingdom of Italy, especially the southern part, it is not so at all, and regarded as a legal and permitted traffic of children. The padrone travels about among the Italian villages, as a peddler does among American villages. Finding a poor family, he offers to apprentice two or more children as harpers or musicians. A legal contract is drawn up, in which he promises to treat the children kindly, even as his own. A small sum is paid at once to the parents, and at the end of three years, a sum is paid the father, about $90 in gold, besides giving the boys a new harp and violin at a value of ten ducats [a ducat is a gold coin found in European countries before World War I] at a value of $8 in gold. If the boys take to themselves one cent of their earnings, the padrone can appropriate ten cents from the money he is bonded to pay the parents. If the boys leave the master, or if he neglects them, each is subject to a fine of $24 and interest.

There are various provisions of the contract, which, in effect, leave the padroni an almost unlimited opportunity of abusing and cheating the unfortunate children. If the little harper is beaten and starved, he has no amends. If he runs away, his family is fined, and it is difficult for him to prove ill-treatment by the master. Besides, he has no means of support. One infamous padrone, well known to the police in Paris and London, given the title of "The Blind," retired with a fortune of 200,000 francs obtained from the hard won earnings of these unfortunate little musicians."

December 10, 1873, New York Times

Dirty ill-clad street children brought in more money tugging at the heartstrings of city inhabitants. The little street musicians played for money in every village square and depressing alley as a part of the ragged barefoot crowd surviving on outdoor relief. They often pilfered food to nourish their semi-savage existence, filching bread begrimed with filth or regaling themselves upon semi-petrified meat bones pulled from garbage piles.

The padrone managed dozens of indentured children taught to play the street organ, violin, or harp, or to put on view trained animals, merely to earn a comfortable living for themselves. The Padrone System, despite its many injustices, was not completely eradicated until the middle of the twentieth century.

II

*"We left Paris for New York in 1871, and were at least
a month on the ocean. I got most of what I ate from the
shakings of the tablecloths from the dining room of the
first-class passengers. One day the cook saw me on the
upper deck of the ship and took me to where he did the
cooking. He gave me beans and pork with white bread,
and immediately after I had eaten, we had a bad
storm at sea, and I was sick! Everyone in our part
of the boat [steerage] was sick, and we were not
allowed to go on the top deck for several days."*

–Johnny

Known overseas as the steady ship, the *La Touraine*, titled after French kings and Renaissance châteaux's, was outfitted with two funnels and four masts. Her twin triple-expansion steam engines powered two propellers that could drive her at 19 knots. On a transatlantic voyage, she was one of a number of ships that had related wireless radio warnings about icebergs to the *RMS Titanic* shortly before that ship's fatal collision. At present, the *La Touraine* held 1,090: Austrians, Hungarians, Bohemians, Croatians, Dalmatians, Greeks, and others, confined to steerage of the transatlantic service on the North Atlantic. On this voyage, no one championed with more *contadini* (peasants) on board than the Italians.

The bottom of the ship swelled with third-class or the well-branded steerage passengers. Hundreds of people crowded together, all sleeping in unchanged clothes alongside their rolled-up belongings. The steerage compartments were nearly five feet high, with two tiers of beds. A narrow, makeshift bed was provided for each person, but looked as if not wide enough for one to turn over. The only vent and light available filtered down through a hatchway, and already the air was filthy and foul with a mix of odors of not-too-clean bodies and the stench of insufficient toilet rooms. This contributed to an atmosphere difficult for any human to endure.

Passengers appeared to be nodding off rather than abandoned to sound sleep. A bare-headed woman wearing a fanciful scarf from Rome or Florence draping her shoulders huddled against an infant while she rocked her frame back and forth in tune with the rhythmic waves of the sea. Quietly, the woman crooned a soothing lullaby to her distressed child, stroking tiny earrings in a daydreaming reverie.

For the first time in their lives, Italians from different parts of Italy found themselves forced to mix with each other in the crowded steerage sections, Sicilians and Neapolitans from various provinces, all speaking different dialects that often their own *paisans* (fellow countryman) could not understand. At home the Northerners looked down on the Southerners because of their lack of education and collective status. The territory extending down from Rome to Sicily, the *Mezzogiorno* ("Midday," for the southern half of the state), produced eighty percent of the Italians that came to America. And yet on the ship crossing the Atlantic, these differences disappeared as they clung together.

Authorized personnel rarely postponed the opportunity to drink in fresh air on the top deck, and passengers were seldom allowed on deck, except for a reserved area situated in the worst part of the ship. This area was subject to violent motion and dirt from the stacks, not to speak of odors from the hold and galleys.

In steerage, one tin saucepan, one tin dipper, a tin spoon, a tin fork, and nothing else could be found on each passenger's bunk. As the immigrants proceeded to the ship's galley to receive their dole, two Italian stewards dispensed the food. The first steward was a dirty middle-aged man in a filthy shirt. His hands were soiled with ship soot, kitchen dirt, and human dirt. He pulled a stale biscuit out of a burlap sack and shoved it onto the plates. Next, he fetched a tin dipper and filled it with coarse red wine handing the cup over. The next man slopped a dipper of thin undercooked *maccheroni* (macaroni) into a tin saucepan. All the passengers followed the return line to a platform on the lower deck, because there were no dining rooms or means of seating provided. The only provisions for eating were in the passages of sleeping compartments, or on the floor. As a result, many took to the floor with others, eating their dish full of macaroni soup while watchfully removing worms and water bugs. With semi-full bellies, the assembly washed gear in a barrel of cold sea water, the same water used to wash the filth from passengers' bodily parts.

The crossing from Europe to America took approximately four weeks. On this particular trip storms raged for three days and nights. The wind, persistently remaining in the northwest, blew a gale impeding the ship. The hatches were closed during the rough weather, making the air increasingly filthy and foul as the journey progressed. People huddled in their berths for most of the voyage, in a stupor caused by the foul air, and nearly all were painfully ill the whole way across. The rough water made their stomachs retch bitter green bile from the hollows of malnourished bellies. They didn't care. They were that sick, and they were that terrified. They talked. They slept. They prayed. A number of them begged to God that the ship would go down as the waves washed over it. Others implored mighty Neptune to carry their bodies out to sea with other lost souls as the squall knocked the vessel about with fury.

On the morning of the fourth day the engines breathed again, the mighty screws churned the quiet sea to foam, and the surging waves remained calm. The wind veered southward and was more favorable as the sun kindled the deck in a blanket of warmth. Hatches were opened and spirits lifted as incoming air wafted away smells from rank toilets and berths soiled with vomit. Several elderly suffered with stiff-man syndrome, their bodies unwilling to give an inch. Others gathered together, conversing in broken English as they studied that new and promising tongue. In a corner several men boasted of how America, the "golden land," meant employment was plentiful, the land was fertile, and there would be plenty to eat. Many anticipated showing profit to either return home or send for their families left behind. Women spoke of their children going to good schools.

In spite of the miserable conditions, most everyone struggled to maintain sanity as the ship pushed forward the balance of the voyage. The day before landing, the immigrants celebrated with song and dance. Many Italians were known musicians. Accordions, harps, *zampogna's* (bagpipe's) with double-chantered pipes, violins and *viola's*, and mandolins were numerous. There were castanets, wood blocks, and tambourines. One man withdrew a *quartara* (pitcher) and blew across an opening in the narrow neck of the ceramic bottle. Soon a couple from Tuscany began to dance a *veloce* (fast dance) to violins and *tambour de basques* (tambourine dance steps), resembling a sprightly *saltarello* (merry dance) as the musicians increased the tempo, testing the twosome's endurance against pairs of heavy clogs.

A hopeful young woman danced the *tarantella*, a fast, upbeat

WAVERLY PUBLIC LIBRARY

whirling dance accompanied by tambourines and telling a story of love in mime. The social gathering continued into the hours of darkness until uneasy sleep fell.

III

"We finally got to Castle Garden in New York,
and had to stay there the larger part of two days and
a night. I was told to call the man by my side Papà.
There seemed to be some trouble about me being
there from authorities, especially when I went
onto the streets to play music and pass the hat."

–Johnny

Foreign cries infused the air with cheering. People kissed family and strangers alike. Tempestuous wonder rose above rugged plank floors that feet stood upon. Hopefulness dawned in the ailing. Quiet tears escaped desperate eyes, and the strong danced in merriment. Then, a sudden silence enveloped the vessel as all eyes concentrated on one supernal vision. As the ship drifted into New York Bay, standing grand with her torch held high, spreading rays of liberty enlightening the world, and casting beacons of hope and adventure, Lady Liberty lifted the heavy spirits of the immigrants as they floated by. Nearly everyone on board was leaving behind one sort of affliction or another: famine, economic depressions, or religious and political punishments. The Lady, however, looked at them as if to say, "Welcome home. Where have you been? Your journey to the land of freedom has come to an end."

No one spoke a word as the ship entered New York harbor. Thousands upon thousands of them had never been away from their own farms and villages before. Each stood alone in thought as their eyes beheld the full of Lady Liberty. She represented a big and powerful country that was to be their future home. They stood on the brink of a new life in a strange new world called America.

Immigrants arriving in the state of New York between August 1, 1855 through April 18, 1890, were required to be processed by the State, and not the Federal government, as they came through Castle Garden [originally known as Castle Clinton, a fort built for the War of 1812] located on the southern tip of Manhattan Island, New York, in Battery Park. Nearly 9 million immigrants passed through Castle Garden constituting the first large wave of immigrants settling and populating the United States. For reasons unknown, Johnny escaped record on the ship's passenger list. In all probability, the young *ragazzos* (boys) were secreted under the hand of the *padroni*.

> "An officer of New York State boarded our ship and took count of passengers, births and deaths at sea, and all kinds of sickness. When we reached shore, the passengers, baggage and all, were taken to Castle Garden, between two lines of officials, in the same manner as railway officials put wild cattle into the cars, minus the whipping. In the registration passage along Castle Garden, we were met by one government official examining us for any signs of sickness missed by health authorities at quarantine. Those discovered sick, blind, crippled, lunatics, and likely to become future charges of the United States, were transferred by steamer to hospitals on Ward's or Blackwell's Island. Another official asked us a set of questions: what is your name, where is your former place of residence, where are you going, what is your trade, and what is your nationality?

Then we were pushed farther on to a large open area in the rotunda where we remained until all passed through.

The Labor Exchange office was useful for those who were not fixed on any particular place, especially for those with no money to carry them further. A meal could be bought for a half dollar for those waiting for employment. There was no place to sleep unless on the floor. One would conclude from the name Castle Garden that we were entering paradise, but I would call it by another name."

Castle Garden, 1871

Castle Garden closed due to progressive immigration from Europe into New York. A new site was located in Upper New York Bay near the New Jersey shore known as Ellis Island. While the new immigration station on Ellis Island was under construction, the Barge Office at the Battery was used for a couple of years to process the immigrants. Ellis Island opened its doors on January 1st, 1892 receiving nearly 500,000 immigrants that same year, but five years later a fire broke out on the island, leaving this building a total loss since it was constructed of pine. Rebuilding started this time using fireproof materials; brick over a steel frame, undergoing a three year construction. On December 17, 1900, a magnificent new 1.5 million dollar station opened its doors.

To appreciate a comparable assessment of the immigrant experience, practice on Ellis Island was fairly rigorous. Shipping companies made large profits carrying "human cargo" to the United States, and bringing cotton, wood, and crop cargoes to Europe and on the return trip. Before leaving Europe, steamship companies prepared an accurate listing of each passenger, along with information about each person, all entered on a formal list. This, the ship's manifest, was used by the captain as a record of inventory of cargo.

The federal government required the shipping companies to

begin the inspection process before an immigrant entered America. If an immigrant had to be sent back to a country of origin, it would be up to the shipping company to bear the cost. After a few days of processing, immigrants were able to buy steerage tickets. They underwent legal, physical, and mental examinations. Before boarding they received vaccinations and were disinfected along with their clothing and baggage at the port. They were bombarded with twenty-nine specific questions about every facet of their lives, and they would repeat every single one of these assessments and more upon arrival at Ellis Island.

Quarantine and medical inspectors boarded the ship in New York harbor, processing and approving all native born Americans and first-class and second-class passengers by means of a passenger list or manifest provided by the ships purser. The ship's doctor advised the checkers of any births or deaths at sea, of those that were sick, and of the names of any passengers taken off by the quarantine officers for contagious diseases such as small pox, yellow or scarlet fever, or measles. Once the ship docked along one of the Hudson River piers, cabin-class passengers went freely down the gangway, collected their bags after customs inspection, and could pass directly into New York City. Their ticket cost could range anywhere from $72 to $400, depending on the choice of rooms. On the other hand, all steerage passengers were taken in barges to Ellis Island for processing. On average, their ticket cost was $30, and larger ships holding from 1,500 to 2,000 immigrants netted a profit of $45,000 to $60,000 for shipping companies for a single, one-way voyage.

With the deck still swaying like ocean waves beneath their feet, the bottom deck passengers proceeded down the gangplank. Crowds of third-class passengers coursed their way toward the main building, with landing tickets and vaccination cards in their caps, hats, and teeth. In the midst of it all, hands filled with babies, suitcases, trunks, cardboard boxes, baskets, leather sacks, and tied fabric bundles gradually made their way to the baggage room, where they were told to check belongings.

While there, they met their first American, an interpreter. The man could speak a minimum of six languages, with more than twelve styles and dialects. Next, a man dressed in the authority of dark blue cloth and threading double rows of brass buttons shouted, "Walk single file up the stairway to the second floor great hall Registry Room." The immigrants moved mechanically. One by one they climbed the steep flight of stairs leading to the Great Hall. Anonymous medical personnel stood at the top of the stairs, watching them for signs of lameness, shortness of breath, heart conditions, and psychological conditions. During the six second examination, observer's looked for any obvious handicaps and deformities. Medical inspection stood between them and a life in America. A man at the bottom of the stairs bellowed, "Men go one way and women and children another. All hats must come off when observing the American flag." Some officials gave a rough shove, shouting in a dozen languages to hurry as they were directed to inspection alleyways, better known as the undignified pens. Matrons, increasingly on the lookout for signs of prostitutes and unwed pregnant women, diverted this group to the Matron's Pen for examination. Women admitting to immoral depravity during questioning could be deported.

Everywhere there were uniforms, watching, and writing, organizing, questioning, and moving. The sounds of shuffling feet and passing traffic grew remote in the immigrants' ears. The smell of disinfectant solidifying the air began to numb them as they came to a bend in the alleyway, causing them to turn. The change in direction gave observers full-body views of front, side, and rear, prompting experienced inspectors to take in six details in one glance: scalp, face, hands, neck, gait, and general condition. Six thousand a day were herded past these doctors, each of which had thirty seconds to judge anything unusual requiring closer examination.

Around the next corner of the path, doctors ordered those filing past to remove gloves, shawls, bonnets, caps, hats, scarves, and handkerchief veils upon their heads, revealing any signs of disease and disability. Floating populations were examined for lice, and if thoroughly invaded, heads were shaved. Others found with a scalp ravaged by favus, a highly inflammatory disease, were marked "SC" on their clothing by physicians wielding the ever-handy piece of chalk. The doctors on Ellis Island had developed a symbolic code for grading immigrants accordingly, and before delivery to the medical room for further examination. One in five immigrants was marked with chalk, indicating a suspected condition. The mark could mean separation from family, a stay in the hospital, or deportation.

> B – Back
> C - Conjunctivitis
> CT – Trachoma
> E – Eyes
> F – Face
> FT – Feet
> G – Goiter
> H – Heart
> K – Hernia
> L – Lameness
> N – Neck
> P – Physical and Lungs
> PG – Pregnancy
> S – Senility
> SC – Scalp (Favus)
> SI – Special Inquiry
> X – Suspected Mental Defect

Silent, watchful, swift, efficient, the doctors examined nearly five thousand a day for the eye disease known as trachoma. To gain additional information on physical health, the physicians used metal instruments known as buttonhooks. With this they rolled back the upper eyelids of each individual, looking for signs of infection. Early outbreaks of the disease alerted steamship companies to conduct trachoma inspections prior to embarking for America, because the disease spread beyond isolated populations. The examination, often repeated on both sides of the ocean, occasionally failed because inspectors ignored washing their hands or instruments in basins of disinfectant.

Penicillin had not yet been invented, and sulphur compounds were no match for the disease. Silver nitrate and a blue stone were used at the island's Immigrant Hospital, the largest Marine hospital in the nation. It was staffed by military surgeons. Eyelids were turned inside out and burned. Copper sulphate painfully stripped diseased tissue away in the hope that healthy tissue would take its place. From time to time individuals with the money to pay first-class ticket rates slipped pleasantly through the procedure. Those found with trachoma in the United States were deported back to their respective countries, but not until cared for at the hospital. Others, surviving recovery, or detained at the hospital for failing mental and mandatory inspection, awaited authorization. Once approved and deemed fit, immigrants could leave the island, passing into America. Still other's died on the island in one of the general psychopathic or contagious disease hospitals, due to lack of antibiotics at the time for fatal diseases of cholera, diphtheria, tuberculosis, and polio. Those dying of infectious diseases were tied up in sheets soaked in disinfectant, their bodies buried in unmarked paupers' graves on Hart's Island or Mt. Olivet in Queens.

The germs of the world merged on Ellis Island. These same

specialists checked the newcomers along the alleyway lines for malaria and typhus from the Tropics, cholera and hookworm from the Mediterranean, and favus and trachoma from Central and Eastern Europe. The incurables and likely public charges were deported and paid by the shipping companies.

Subsequent to the Registry Room, a uniformed Immigration's Bureau member stamped health cards before sending people onto the Primary Inspection Room. Here the immigrant learned if he would be allowed into America or not. With the help of an interpreter, he was asked twenty-nine questions. His answers were essential to matching the primary manifest when leaving their countries.

1. What is your number on the list?
2. What is your name in full?
3. How old are you?
4. What is your sex?
5. Are you married or single?
6. What is your occupation?
7. Can you read and write?
8. What is your nationality?
9. What is your race?
10. Where was your last residence giving country and city or town?
11. What is the name and address of a relative in your native country?
12. What is your final destination in the US?
13. Into which US seaport have you landed?
14. Do you have a ticket to your final destination?
15. Who paid your passage?
16. How much money is in your possession? More or less than $30?
17. Have you ever been in the US before?
18. Are you going to join a relative? What relative? Name? Address?

19. Have you ever been in prison, an almshouse institution for the insane, or poorhouse supported by charity?
20. Are you a Polygamist?
21. Are you an Anarchist?
22. Do you have an offer promise, or an agreement of labor in the US?
23. What is the condition of your health?
24. Are you deformed in anyway or crippled?
25. What is your height?
26. What is your complexion?
27. What is the color of your hair and eyes?
28. Do you have any identifying marks on your body?
29. Where is the place of your birth?

Those settlers making their way through Ellis Island bought tickets for a thousand places in America. At the Money Exchange counter in the main building they traded their liras, rubles, zlotys, and marks for dollars before arriving at the Stairs of Separation, three screened-off stairs leading to different locations pointing toward the future. On the left was the Stairway to the New York Ferry, for those free to reach Manhattan. On the right was the Stairway to the Railroad Barges, for immigrants who were free to leave and travel via the railroad station in Jersey City. In the center was the Stairway to Temporary Detention, for immigrants bound for the information bureau to solve manners of difficulty. In the Special Inquiry Detention Room three inspectors were required to take note of every immigrant needing further investigation. The board had the power to admit an immigrant—or to exclude one ordering deportation. Appeals came in varied ways.

Health issues, criminal records, and no means of support, to mediocre testimony before the board officials there. "I caught this boy in the Mess Hall gulping an entire pitcher of milk. He stuffed his belly with ice cream, mounds of bread and butter, and ate the banana, skin and all. He said he had never seen a banana before. I asked for his landing card, his inspection card, his health card, and he could produce none. He came ashore as a stowaway, sir. An illegal on free soil."

On occasion, the spelling of an immigrant's name met with alterations, due to nationality language gaps in the pronunciation of certain letters in the alphabet. But more frequently, after the immigrant was processed into American culture, second-generation and third-generation families adopted Americanized names and changed name spellings.

From 1892, until Ellis Island officially closed its doors in 1954, some 12 million people were to follow through this port of entry into the United States. From inception to finale, an exodus of sixty-two years turned away only two percent of the more than twelve million people from Ellis Island. Scores of Europe's blood turned out to be industrious, patriotic, and farsighted citizens. On land once empty, they planted, built, mined, and toiled with their hands. They loved their new motherland and appreciated the blessings she furnished.

IV

*"We were released after a while at Castle Garden,
and went to an apartment house [tenement] where we
had only two rooms. We went on the streets to play our
instruments and pass the hat. Sometimes I got back to
the room, and sometimes I slept on doorsteps."*

–Johnny

Each immigrant discovered his or her own, unique New York. In the neighborhood below Fourteenth Street of *Piccola Italia* (Little Italy) on the Lower East Side of Manhattan, many Italians—afraid of being separated from other Italians upon entering the great city—settled among their own kind. Even if it meant living in a dark and dirty city tenement, here everyone clamored together. Frightened to venture beyond familiar streets and untutored in the English vocabulary, they were wary of strangers and heeded constant rumors that kept some unsettled. The Italians were often pilloried with insulting names such as wop, dago, guinea, and sneaky bandits of assassins. Others were charged with pauperism, crime, and degraded living. Yet these short and sturdy laborers who swung along the streets with their heavy strides early in the morning and late at night worked in sweatshops, experiencing deplorable conditions. They were underpaid and overworked, suffering through poor ventilation and hazardous conditions. Former generations had been luckier, working as independent merchants selling fruit from handcarts in the city streets, or as longshoremen and construction workers, often under the guidance of the padrone (labor boss) finding work for the new immigrants, securing them jobs upon arrival to American shores.

⚜

Bottle Alley onto the "Bend" in Mulberry Street, where mulberry trees once grew on Broadway, was in the neighborhood of the Five Points House of Industry, an eight-story building suited for the indigent. Rags blew on the clotheslines overhead and hawkers offered a worn coat for fifty cents. A group of people mutter in foreign tongues, taking the strain off family life. Children were duty bound to scour the streets looking to find spare pieces of coal for fuel. People passed. Big dirty boys jostled and shoved, raucous and laughing. On a plank laid across two ash barrels, piles of fish lay rotting in the sun. No musicians played here, for there was no one to throw pennies to them in the midst of jagged brick and rusted pots existing as playthings for a crowd of dirty children romping about on rigid black earth in front of ramshackle buildings.

New York City lived with the constant threats of epidemics, because the steady numbers of immigrants that needed places to live allowed for excessive rents of ten to twelve dollars a month, to be paid by those who earned an average monthly wage of thirty dollars. Children slept on worn steps damaged by long use crossing the threshold of a sunless two-room flat, occupied at various times with ten persons of both sexes and all ages. Two beds stood without partitions in the dark and unhealthy rooms, and bedbugs were commonplace in the shared space. A table stood with five chairs, and a sofa sat in the kitchen, gainfully used as a makeshift bed. Dark wainscoting, scratched and chipped, hung with damp yellow clothes, plaster falling at all times. When pipes froze in the winter, there was no drinking water for days, and in the summer oppressive heat lead to rats, flies, sickness, and the stench of consuming waste.

Serious illness used up the bulk of numerous immigrants. For many, the East-side killer seized them as the pink-petal flush, coupled with eyes of peculiar luminous beauty, were both as typical as the cough in the confines of tenement living, before victims surrendered to tuberculosis. Poverty, their badge and typical condition, invited and compelled the poor man's destruction. Cholera, yellow fever, tuberculosis, and typhus led many tenement souls to paupers' graves.

Perplexed by conflict and old hopes, the children of the street went about peddling newspapers along blocks of tidy brownstones climbing behind neat squares of lawn and iron fences. They polished shoes, ran errands, carried satchels to steamboat docks, and canvassed the East River waterfront in the hope of picking up odd jobs. In Italy a boy would be detected as a *scugnizzi* (street urchin). In America he was branded a guttersnipe, urchin, and waif of the city, bumming and stealing his way toward survival. In the midst of gnawing hunger, he often slept curled up in a box or on the pavement over printing house vaults, where the heat would impart some warmth to his half-clad and chilled limbs. Often the gutter was his horizon.

❧

"One evening the other boys wandered into a large department store. I was following them, but when I got out onto the street there was no one I knew, so I went back inside the store. I didn't see anyone I knew there either, so I

went out onto the street again and simply wandered along.
I walked until I was tired, not knowing where I was going.
Finally, I came to a small candy and pool room. There
was a little couch by the wall, so I sat there, and at length
fell asleep. When I awakened I started to go out onto the
street, but a man motioned me back to the couch.
He covered me up with a tattered coat, and in the
morning he gave me some breakfast. Later he brought an
Italian boy over to talk with me as I spoke little English,
and told me I could stay there nights until I found my way
home. Eventually, the man took me to a place for
lost people, but no one came after me. I stayed there
several days, and then I was turned over to the
Children's Aid Society of New York City."

–Johnny

Born in Litchfield, Connecticut, Charles Loring Brace, philanthropist, New York Times editorial writer, author, and Protestant minister turned social worker, founded the New York Children's Aid Society in 1853.

From its beginning, the work of the Children's Aid Society involved several efforts. The most radical and well-known was the "emigration plan," the "placing out system," or what has become known as the "orphan trains." Brace's plan to send children away from the over-populated city streets to find them family homes in the West was triggered by the tumultuous times after the Civil War and of newly arrived immigrants anticipating a better life than the squalor of tenement poverty in which they lived. The result had wrought thirty-thousand children running rampant on the streets of New York City, while infanticide gave way to scattered human remains. Brace cited the death of one or both parents or ill-treatment that left many children to fend on their own.

Children were often preyed on by immoral individuals who sent them out to steal, sell, or play hand organs or other musical devices for money helping those in the trade of exploiting to profit. Boys sold newspapers or hawked matches, while many girls were forced into prostitution. Brace considered these children the dangerous classes and their multiplying numbers ultimately a threat to all of society, yet he believed that if he could show these children that someone cared enough about them, and to educate them in good habits of industry and self-control, and help them achieve some basic skills, they could get jobs and improve their lives. He felt that "home life was better than institutions and that self-help was better than alms."

In the first forty years, Brace's relocation experiment sent 97,738 children from New York by train to nearly every state in the union. The bulk of these children resided within eastern states, followed by multitudes distributed across the Midwest. The placing-out system designed by Brace was unique, but he was also driven by religious and idealized views of the West, where there were "good Christian homes and many spare places at the table of life." Brace felt the endeavor positive. "The effort to place the children of the street in country families revealed a spirit of humanity and kindness, throughout the rural districts, which was truly delightful to see." Yet the harsh realities of farming and rural life were unfamiliar to him. While some children became members of these families and gained from the experience, others were put to work in stores and on farms, in conditions similar to indentured servitude.

Since Brace could not remove every poor child from the bad influences of the city, he also made local efforts. These included thirteen night schools, twenty-one day or industrial schools, and seven newsboys lodging homes, five country health charities, including the Brace Farm School at Valhalla in Westchester County where boys would gain knowledge in basic agricultural training before transport to the West. The lodging houses were places a homeless child could come so a boy or girl did not have to sleep on the street. A young person could stay for a night or two if his difficulty was temporary, or he could stay for extended periods, and be assured of receiving food, wash and shelter. If children could pay, they were asked for a small sum so that they felt they were paying their own way, rather than accepting charity. These lodging houses eventually offered evening or morning classes to help the children with reading and writing, and specific skills that could help them gain employment.

The Children's Aid Society also operated a "Family Emigration Program" through which they provided train tickets for entire families to rejoin a wage earner who had found work in another state, for example, or paid a portion of the fare to return to Europe. The CAS had occasionally provided help for entire families from its earliest days, but the records of the Family Emigration Program date from 1874-1926.

The Orphan Train movement [1854-1929] and the success of initiatives led to a host of child welfare reforms, including child labor laws, adoption and the establishment of foster care services, public education, the provision of health care and nutrition and vocational training.

There were numerous agencies nationwide that placed children from orphanages on trains to go to foster homes as that was the mode of transportation, but in America, only those children placed from the East Coast, in particular New York, belong to the era of the orphan trains. Besides the New York Children's Aid, other agencies that placed children on orphan trains included the Children's Village in Dobbs Ferry, New York (then known as the New York

Juvenile Asylum), the New York Foundling (then known as the New York Foundling Hospital), the Graham-Windham Home for Children (then known as the Orphan Asylum Society of the City of New York.) In Boston, Home for Wayward Children, and the Baldwin Home for Little Wanderers, to name a few.

"Mr. Eli Trott, an agent of the Aid Society, took me to his home outside the city, and kept me there for some time. After that, Mr. Trott made me understand that I was going away and not coming back [to New York.] He took me to the Aid Society, and while there, I was given a new outfit of clothes. The only possession I had with me when they took me was my triangle, but they kept that."

–Johnny

Eli Trott, born in England, was one of many western agents employed by the Children's Aid Society. Working as both a placing agent of children, and as the superintendent of the Girls Lodging house [later to become the Elizabeth Home for Girls in Manhattan] Mr. Trott's epitaph from *The Yonkers Statesman* read as:

"Eli Trott, aged 87, was prominent in Westchester County as a prohibitionist and a philanthropist, died Thursday night, January 1, 1920 at his home at 25 Audrey Avenue, Mount Vernon, New York. He was a resident of Mount Vernon for fifty years, and was the oldest Deacon of the Baptist Church.

In 1894, he ran for Mayor of this city, on the Prohibition ticket. Mr. Trott was an agent for the Children's Society of

Manhattan fifty-four years, and in that time placed 5,500 children in institutions. For sixteen years, he was Treasurer of the Baptist Chautauqua Society. He is survived by his wife Mary (first wife Lois, a teacher and matron of the Girls Lodging House, died in 1894) a son, Cyrus, and a daughter, Eloise. The interment will be in Woodlawn Cemetery."

Another agent, Charles R Fry, Superintendent of the Children's Summer Home in Bath Beach, Long Island, spent many years as the resident representative of emigration for the Children's Aid Society. As a child rescuer shepherding abandoned and orphaned New York children to new homes in the west on orphan trains, Fry was a dedicated social worker looking after the interests of children sent west as well as preparing them for future expeditions. On May 12, 1872, propositioning a crowd of orphans, half-orphans, and other destitute children inside the office building of the Children's Aid Society an agent inquired, "How many of you children who have no parents would love to have nice homes in the West, where you can drive horses and have as many apples and melons as you wish to eat? A place where you'll be able to drink in fresh air and admire panoramic scenes of vast trees and hills and sunsets, cows and horses. There truly are places like this, and there are families in the West just waiting for you to call their own."

"How'd you git here?" one boy whispered to another. "I lived in one a dem newsboy's homes. I paid my way fer a bed at night an had tree squares a day. I could sell me poipers all day 'fore the copper's chased me down da alley like a scart dog. Yea shoulda seen dem coppers til dey caught up wid me. Dey took me in, and did for me without a cap to me head, or shoes to me feet, thin dey dropped me here."

A voice from somewhere in the room burst out, "How will

dey know we're comin?"

"News flyers are sent out to every part of America announcing when and where a trainload of orphans will arrive," the man explained. "Our agents have set up screening committees in various towns along the way where prospective parents can meet and choose a child. These folks may pay you for work, and some will adopt you as their own children."

Another inquired, "What if nobody wants us?"

And yet another murmured nearby, "I gotta ma, but she works out. Couldn't keep me or my brudders and sisters after our pa died."

The children were made ready for the journey--- properly clothed from head to foot with new hats, shoes, and dapper overcoats. One boy gave a shrug and asked another, "Did yer get new underclothes too?"

Fidgeting with anticipation the boy replied, "Yea, dey gave 'em to all da boys. Dey's as stiff as a board. Yer can't feel your behind."

> 1872 - " After a period of neglect and abuse by a *padroni*, and a victim of the padrone system, which the Children's Aid Society and others helped end, seven-year-old Jean Assers, a French boy [residing in Italy] became lost, and by chance was found and cared for by our agent, Mr. E. Trott. Jean went west with a company of children under the supervision of our western agent, Charles R. Fry, to Cresco, Iowa, and was placed with Mr. & Mrs. O. Mildrum in Riceville, Mitchell County, Iowa."

Wanted Homes for Children

A company of orphan and homeless children of different ages in charge of an agent will arrive at your town on date herein mentioned. The object of the coming of these children is to find homes in your midst, especially among farmers, where they may enjoy a happy, wholesome family life. Where kind care, good example, and moral training will fit them for a life of self-support and usefulness. They come under the auspices of the New York Children's Aid Society. They have been tested and found to be well-meaning boys and girls anxious for homes.

The conditions are that these children shall be properly clothed, treated as members of the family, given proper school advantages, and remain in the family until they are eighteen years of age. At the expiration of the time specified it is hoped that arrangements can be made whereby they may be able to remain in the family indefinitely. The Society retains the right to remove a child at any time for just cause, and agrees to remove any found unsatisfactory after being notified. Remember the time and place. All are invited. Come out and hear the address. Applications may be made to any one of the well-known citizens who have agreed to act as a local committee to aid the agent in securing homes.

The Children's Aid Society
105 East 22nd Street
New York, New York

Children were given away for trial periods; the foster family or the orphan could decide at any time if the arrangement was not going well and seek a home elsewhere.

❧

The orphan trains stopped at more than forty-five states across the country as well as Canada. During the early years, Indiana received the largest number of children. Two boys placed in Indiana embrace unique experiences.

While at a train stop in Tipton, Senator John Green had called out to the procession of children standing before him for the most "ragged and friendless" in the lot. A boy named Jack was presented. Jack had been picked up off the New York City streets starving in Chatham Square one frosty night. He in fact begged a policeman to arrest him. Anything was better than returning to his motherless home along the East River and Roosevelt Street, where his father "flogged him sorely" for not bringing in enough money from selling newspapers. Jack was sent with a boatload of other waifs to Randall's Island. While there, Theodore Roosevelt, Sr. (father of the U.S. 26th President, and a developing founder of the New York Children's Aid Society,) rescued Jack and turned him over to the Society.

"Good day," he began as he doffed his hat looking like one of the fine quills walking down Broadway. "My name is Senator John Green," the man from Indiana spoke with the authority of experience. Observing the boy, the man thought he was the scrawniest, toughest looking, and most unpromising of the lot of motley youngsters. A real challenge. He had a curious desire to see what could be made of such an example of humanity and took him home. The senator, one day to become judge, contended, "I trust with fresh air, butter, and eggs, we can remedy the shortfall."

The disheveled boy appreciated his home and the kindness of his benefactors, and consciously applied himself to study. From public school to Waveland Academy, to four years study at Yale, Jack went to England pursuing an education in theology. Many years later, the lad, John (James) Green Brady, went to Alaska as a missionary under the Presbyterian Church educating the Indians, and established the Sitka Trading Company. While in Alaska, President William McKinley appointed John Brady the fifth governor of Alaska. Once, at a conference in Portland, Oregon, Brady approached young Theodore Roo-

sevelt, the son of his rescuer, who, at the time, was governor of
New York.

> "*Governor Roosevelt, the other governors have greeted
> you with interest, simply as a fellow governor and a great
> American, but I greet you with infinitely more interest, as
> the son of your father, the first Theodore Roosevelt.*" When
> greeted warmly by Governor Roosevelt and asked why and
> in what special way he had been interested in his father,
> Governor Brady replied, "*Your father picked me up on the
> streets of New York, a waif and an orphan, and sent me to
> a Western family, paying for my transportation and early
> care. Years passed and I was able to repay the money which
> had given me my start in life, but I can never repay what he
> did for me, for it was through that early care and by giving
> me a foster mother and father that I gradually rose in the
> world, and now I greet his son as a fellow governor as a part
> of our great country.*"
>
> *Wikipedia – Theodore Roosevelt*

Meanwhile coincidence had been at work with Andrew
E Burke, another child of the streets. Deserted by his father and
mother, the New York City boy lived by selling newspapers and boot
blacking. One night, while young Andy was finding shelter inside a
dry goods box, he was discovered by the police, and gathered in with
other outcasts. On August 31, 1859, Andy Burke and Johnny Brady,
and twenty-five other New York waifs started West in the care of the
Children's Aid Society.

Burke's early path lay far apart to that of his train companion.
He did not reap the benefits of a loving foster home, and enlisted as a
drummer boy at the age of twelve with the 75th Indiana Infantry in
the American Civil War of 1862. Later, working his way off his foster

parent's farm in Noblesville, Andrew found work as a cashier in a neighboring town. After serving a term as county treasurer, young Andy moved to North Dakota. He succeeded so well, that when the territory became a state, Andrew Burke was elected the second governor of North Dakota.

※

"The next morning we took the ferry boat to the railroad station. There I could have gone to an apartment where the folks (with whom I had lived) were, but I was put on a train and started for the West. The older boys had lots of fun getting me to tell them stories. They couldn't understand what I said, but they laughed and clapped their hands. I remember crossing the Niagara River. The train stopped on the bridge and we saw the falls."

–Johnny

The children's imaginations reached to vast stretches of tree-dotted fields and waving grass in the breeze as they assembled for placing in the West. Little did they know that one day they would become a part of history involving the largest mass migration of children ever to take place upon American soil.

Young children riding the trains never really knew the meaning of losing any means of contacting their relatives in New York, if they had them. They were never to speak, or think of their families again. They were to completely start over with new families. The older children would remember their old lives, nostalgias often heightened by the coming of age. Bitterness often faded, but not the sense of loss. Some would wake up in the hot summer nights of new homes and for a few moments think they were in Sicily or Ireland or Minsk. Some would think their mothers were at the fireplace in the next room, preparing food—the old food—the food of the Old Country. The babies would have no memory of their former existence.

As steel wheels set in motion the wood burning 4-4-0 steam locomotive, the children observed "The Lady" far beyond their window seats. They may have sensed she was bidding them farewell and good luck to new adventures. Around seven hours into the trip one of the two agents traveling with the group announced an impressive stopover along the water-level route following the north Lake Erie shoreline. "We will cross the Niagara River soon and stop a few minutes on the bridge to see Niagara Falls. No one will leave the train, but you will have ten minutes of viewing the majestic Falls of Niagara from your seats."

Ooos and ahs erupted from open mouths of every shape and size as all eyes gazed upon a voluminous and sublime natural wonder. One boy elbowed another, "How'd yea like ta fall in a drink like dat."

The train parted some of the children in Ontario, Canada before chugging down the flat raceway of the main line of New York Central's Canadian Southern Railroad route traveling north of three Great Lakes in the direction of Detroit, Michigan, yielding a station stop taking on water in track pans. Excess water blasted out of the relief vents on the tender deck as the exchange to the Michigan Central Railroad [a wholly owned subsidiary of the New York Central] train moved on to Battle Creek where the journey for others came to an end.

Lined up in a string, the children stood the stage in the town hall. The agent began the address, telling the crowd standing before him the plight of the children and the saving work the Children's Aid Society performs. He announced all interested parents must sign papers with one of the local screening committees. He informed all that an agent of the society would remain in the area for a day or two visiting the homes in which children had been placed. Moving along, the agent stood to the side of each child, giving out information on each to spectators. The introductions continued until all the children were initiated, then the crowd flocked the stage like vultures ready to pick their possessions. Some folks poked at the older boys' muscles, judging them fit for farm labor. Other's acted upon teeth examinations for the reason that some children might cost money for needed dental work. Siblings wailed as families separated them, pulling them in different directions. The children were poked, prodded, shoved, and jabbed. They were hugged, cuddled, and kissed.

The train followed rivers, with no significant grades up to now. Not catching sight of cows and horses, as promised by the sign-up speech, restrained doubt in the children's minds remained until the steamer took a curve in the bend beyond a grove of trees. Squeals of excitement erupted as all clamored closer to the windows, some projecting themselves midpoint into open air while viewing cattle and horses grazing on distant rolling green hills, among fields of crops, in pastures, and along woodlands. One boy cried out, "Ride 'em cowboy!" Most had glimpsed only pictures in a book of cows and horses. Apples, once pocketed from vending carts in the New York streets, now appeared on trees, ornamenting them in generous reds. Looking back through the door window they saw beds of wild flowers, and beyond that, rail fences, and former paddocks. The wide open spaces of the western prairie appeared natural—purely man and land.

Jaded into sleep by the clickety-clack of steel wheels passing over jointed tracks, the children dozed. Over the course of the past two days into the heartland, where they were fed and, in turn, put on display for prospective adopters, some slept uneasily as crowded thoughts invaded visions of what their futures held.

⁂

"After traveling for several days we came to Chicago.
I remember the buildings were still black from the big fire."

–Johnny

Wild geese coursed westbound, the train shining a light through the cool Illinois rain, as wheels propelled by ribs of steel skirted the blackened remains of the LaSalle Street Station in Chicago moving forward to Capital Depot. Winsome faces bent far-reaching looks beyond the train windows to gaze upon a scene of incomplete buildings charred and crestfallen, a city, even now, exhibiting signs of ruin.

Southwest winds the night of October 8th, had been gusting to thirty miles per hour. Many homes in Chicago, at the time made of wood and poorly constructed, surrounded sidewalks and roads also made of wood. Rainfall that summer had been scant, and for the three weeks leading up to October 8, 1871, no rain had fallen. That night a fire tore through four square miles, more than 2,000 acres, and destroying 17,000 buildings. Nearly 300,000 residents lost their homes, and 300 people died. The one thing that helped stop the great Chicago three-day fire was the rainstorm the following day.

Ordinarily, the children traveling farther west, from the upper Midwest, were expected to change train lines in Chicago; those traveling further west, from the lower Midwest, changed in St. Louis. The agent instructed the children to wash up once inside the building and change into new garments. Boys in knickers and blouses, girls in dresses, before making their way to the stage. At this, the older children felt a deep pit gnawing away in their stomachs as they went through the motions of readiness. Some of the children sang songs while others danced, exhibiting eye-catching footwork that attracted the attention of new mothers and fathers for quick selection. The children did not have to go with those who selected them if they didn't want to, but the agents also told them they might not get another chance with a family along the way. The unselected would return to New York to work, or try again for another placing.

VI

*"We went on to Prairie du Chien, Wisconsin,
and stayed overnight there before taking the
ferry across to McGregor, Iowa in the morning.
From McGregor we went on by train, and at
noon reached Cresco in Howard County Iowa.
Seven of us, six boys and a small girl, were taken to the
courthouse where we were taken in by different families."*

–Johnny

As sure as a bird flies in the sky above, the train moved onto Prairie du Chien, Wisconsin. The trip was getting long for all of them. The few short stretches the children took—other than being on display for possible selection—were at whistle stops for coal, wood, and water. Preparations were made at suitable points along the route for fresh provisions to be sent into the car on the arrival of the train. The children did not leave the car except on the few occasions when a change of train was necessary. Mustard sandwiches were doled out at this point, and metal cups filled with warm Wisconsin milk were consumed, filling bellies and putting the children under sedation.

In the morning, seven children ferried across the muddy water from Prairie du Chien, Wisconsin, to McGregor, Iowa, located along the Mississippi River connecting Lake Michigan with the Mississippi River by rail. Clammers nearby gazed at the children while managing the shore anticipating prospective trade of shells and pearls to a button industry; keeping an ever watchful eye out for that big pearl that would make them rich. Once in McGregor, the children boarded the Milwaukee and Prairie du Chien short line, an outgrowth of an early Milwaukee Road of the McGregor Western railroad, taking them on to Cresco, the county seat of Howard County, Iowa.

As the children walked into a stylish, red brick courthouse, trimmed with Milwaukee brick of a soft cream color, shhs echoed throughout the room like the noise of steam escaping a pressurized valve. Johnny, dressed in stiff collar and cuffs, sensed this was his last chance at finding a home. The train agent gave the usual speech, and a large crowd waited in line to see and inspect the children. It seemed all Iowans wanted a child, and there weren't enough children left on the train to go around.

A heavy, strong, and muscular farmer approached one boy.

"Oh, you'd make a good hand on the farm," he said as he palmed the boy's arm.

"Wot's dat awful stink? I taint goin home wid you. You smell like you taint had a bath in a yer," the boy said pinching his nose.

The farmer took the boy by the arm, leading him down the great hall, when the boy bit and kicked the man, fleeing quickly from his hold. Each person in the crowd witnessing the disturbance thought the boy incorrigible. No prospective parents came near him. After all, many rural folk were predisposed to view the children with suspicion, as out of control offspring of drunkards and prostitutes. The children spoke with the accents of Ireland, Germany, and Italy, and the colloquial speech of New York slang. One man in the crowd challenged, "What was good for New York is very bad for the West.

Bad blood and heathens is what they are!"

Near the corner of the street Johnny could see halfway down the block, where children and suitcases were loaded into wagons and carriages taking them on to towns where their new families lived. Johnny set out for Jamestown Township in Howard County, Iowa.

❧

> *"Mr. Mildrum took me. He lived a mile and a half east*
> *of Riceville, Iowa on a farm in Jamestown Township.*
> *My age was supposed to be 7. Mr. and Mrs. Mildrum*
> *were formerly from New England, and were well educated*
> *and highly cultured. I stayed on this farm two years*
> *and learned to speak English, and to read and*
> *spell before I could go to school."*
>
> *–Johnny*

Orrin Mildrum, a highly educated and cultured New Englander from Middletown, Connecticut, had come to Iowa as a single man to dabble in farming and the tinsmith business. It was not unusual for many Iowans to work a business and farm. While holding the position of justice of the peace in Jamestown, Orrin decided to travel back to his native Connecticut to seek a refined wife. There he found former Mount Holyoke Seminary schoolteacher, Julia North, in Waterbury, located twenty miles from the educator's birth town of Berlin. After spending some time with their Eastern families, Orrin brought his new bride to Iowa in 1865.

"What's your name?" a pleasant woman asked Johnny.

"Jean Assers (Zhahn Ashers)," confirmed the lad.

"No, that name won't do. From now on, your name will be

John Mildrum Arsarers (Arser-ers)," she announced. And so it was.

Johnny instantly had an invented name, which in time changed to Arsers, remaining throughout his impending family's lineage.

Johnny liked the Mildrums, a childless couple in their late thirties. He sensed life in Iowa would never cause him the gnawing hunger he often experienced living on the streets of New York. Here bountiful fields of wheat stretched to the horizon, and oats and corn spread throughout the landscape. The boy reflectively reviewed the scenes of his early life, replacing tenements with farms dotting the countryside. He beheld beautiful areas of sloping timber of jack oak, burr oak, poplar, and basswood, while alternating woods of elm, maple, and butternut sandwiched between. A brook, known by the settlers as the Little Wapsie, flowed south about midway through Jamestown township associated with an urban city Riceville; existing within two counties, Mitchell and Howard. Settlers coming from Wisconsin and Eastern states crossed the river at McGregor or Dubuque. They then proceeded west by way of Decorah, Cresco and Riceville and on into Mitchell and Howard Counties, where the Mildrums lived. Most of those who settled here were from New York and the New England states, but the state's ethnic populations scored high in German, followed by Swedes, Norwegians, and English. Johnny sensed he would like Iowa. No *padroni* were near to make him feel unsafe.

Farm work appeared to be dictated by the seasons. Wintertime meant butchering, fence mending, ice cutting, and wood chopping. In the spring, farmers prepared and planted their fields. Summertime brought sheep shearing, haying, and threshing. In the fall, farmers picked corn, the most difficult farm task of all, but Orrin and Julia Mildrum were improvers, the ones who adopted crop rotation farming, where a sustainable permanent culture is established. Those who prospered used big names like Deere and McCormick applied to the soil rich in dark loam churned from the sod of virgin prairie, and Johnny became educated in rural life. One of his chores was to herd the cattle to the barn, because there were hungry wolves and other wild animals out at night that could harm the valuable cows. Johnny, ever the adventurous type, had reservations about untamed nature roaming in the West, and Orrin gave Johnny a tin penny whistle. "Blow it if you should ever face danger, and someone will come running to find you." Instead, Orrin found Johnny amid the pasture fields piping out whistle tunes of jigs and reels. His audience, the cows, seemed to enjoy the melody as they stood nearby, happily chewing their cuds.

Julia also adapted to farm life, unlike her eastern education. She became skilled in churning butter, making sauces from the golden pumpkins that grew in her garden, and using Indian corn meal as a flour staple when ground wheat was unavailable. During the winter she sewed and mended and helped with butchering. In spring she cared for newly hatched chicks, planted gardens, and did spring housekeeping. During the summer she canned large amounts of vegetables and fruit and stored apples and potatoes for winter use.

VII

"I started school at age 9, and my first teacher was
Harriet Cook from New Oregon, near Cresco.
I went to school winters, and occasionally in the
spring terms. I never knew Iowa could be so cold."

–Johnny

Julia taught Johnny to speak fluent English and to read and spell, long before placing him in winter school. But Julia was never quite convinced that Johnny would turn out to be a "brilliant scholar." Written within letters sent to her parents and siblings living in Connecticut and New York, Julia expressed:

> "I think Johnny has finished his letter to you three different times. Of course I know you can't read it, but I do not tell him so, nor do I encourage him to send letters unless I am writing. Johnny has been scribbling on paper with a lead pencil, and now he thinks he must use his blotter. He is trying to print a letter to the Aid Society in New York. I have never told him when the Society writes inquiring about him, because I do not want to hear him talk about it. I made the mistake of reading to him the Society's last letter, and he wants to write them back immediately.

He is not very bright at his books, and I am afraid he never will be. His mind is very peculiarly constituted, and we can hardly tell what he will make of himself. He will come home from school and repeat whole sentences from the older scholars Reading and Grammar lessons, but he learns to read very slowly, though I must contend he is a good speller and good in arithmetic. He goes to school in Riceville, and he thinks I am hard on him because he can't go to school at 7 a.m. and stay till 7 p.m. I am afraid he will never make a brilliant scholar. In fact, I'm afraid he will never be very brilliant in anything.

I dread taking him to Riceville as he wants to run the streets the whole time, and of course he can't, so I expect he will grow discontented. Johnny was very much delighted with your mention of him in your letter. He is very fond of being noticed, but it does not answer to make too much of him as it puffs him up uncomfortably. He has been extra good for several days. I try to impress upon him that bad behavior is displeasing to God. Sunday night he was helping me with some work, and inquired if he had been a good boy. I told him yes and praised him for it, when to my astonishment he remarked, "I guess God must be well pleased with me. Don't you think mama?" He is a funny boy, and I can hear him singing to himself in the morning as he is dressing. I don't know what that boy will ever make of himself!"

–Jule

Johnny went to and from school with other children, encumbering a flat-bed wagon. When the snow dampened travel difficulties, horse-drawn passenger sleighs gave them transport.

Every morning upon entering the one-room classroom filled with desks, benches, a potbelly stove, and children of all ages at different levels of instruction, Johnny bowed to Miss Cook, his teacher. This was the way boys made their manners known. The girls would curtsy.

Chester Winfield's father worked the nearly depleted coal mines in Iowa, and the family lived a meager life. In the spring Chester laid shoes aside and tramped through the long prairie grass with only nature's covering on his feet, arriving at school clad in homespun butternut jeans, a trouser dyed brown in the juice of butternut husks. Come winter term, saved boots broke out, protecting his feet from the elements. Chester disliked Johnny immediately and name called him every chance he could get. One day, on the playground a *tauromachian* (bull fight) broke out.

Chester called Johnny a "grape stomping macaroni," and this time Johnny fought back, planting a right fist into Chester's left jaw. Chester countered with a right uppercut to Johnny's chin. The boys rolled and scuffled next to crusty snow clinging to patches of frozen ground. The crowd of school children cheered on Johnny, as Chester was a known bully. The boys continued to punch at each other until Miss Cook, hearing the racket from her classroom, doubled up her skirts and ran for them. The boys were cut and bleeding by the time their teacher arrived at the battle zone. They were told to clean up using a nearby water pail and report to "the closest." All the children knew this was a shameful punishment.

The diminutive storeroom was big enough to hold a few clothing articles, a mop, and a bucket. Both boys stood together in the confined closet space for one hour as punishment. The duo privately thought the usual twenty minutes of after-school detainment a far better punishment than their present situation.

At the outset, the closet was silent, until twenty minutes passed, and Chester's legs grew weak from standing. He squirmed about, seeking a seating arrangement upon the floor, but the tight spaces and Chester's full size wouldn't allow for the exchange.

"Come on, Chester, just a little while longer and we will be out of here soon and can go home. You can do it, I know you can!" Johnny whispered.

"I can't put up with this much longer, I'm claustrophobic!" he declared as his invisible face collected beads of moisture in the closet's darkness.

Johnny didn't know why, but at the moment within the solitude of confined obscurity, he felt the need to bear his soul. He told Chester of the *padroni* and his arrival in America, and Chester absorbed every detail with profound interest. He acquainted his cell mate with his life on the streets of New York, and his ultimate trip west on an orphan train. Then Miss Cook opened the door. The classroom was empty of children.

"I have written a letter to your parent's and expect prompt delivery," she alleged, thrusting parchment into each of their hands. "Your punishment at home will be far worse than this, I venture to say."

As the boys veered off in separate directions, Chester yelled, "You're alright, Johnny boy. You're alright." In the course of the following winter school terms, Chester became Johnny's strongest ally. At all times Chester had Johnny's back if anyone threw a critical remark his way. Chester merely gave "the look," pounding one fist into the palm of the other, and no one wanted to receive what Chester might deliver on the other end. Johnny didn't need Chester's support. The kids liked him. But he was happy just the same to find a friend in Chester.

❦

The weather had been terribly cold in northern Iowa, but on

January 7, 1873, the day had been unusually warm for the season, though without sunshine. A great many residents of Iowa and Minnesota were away from home, including Julia Mildrum. Earlier, Orrin had harnessed Becky and Fan [team of horses] and drove Julia over to the home of friend and allopathic physician, Dr. and Mrs. Wells. The trio intended on going to a prayer meeting in the evening set by Mr. Harvey, the Congregational minister of the church the Mildrum's attended. Johnny arrived home from school nearing 4:00 o'clock, just as Wheeler, the Mildrum's hired hand, was about to start chores. "Bundle up," he told Johnny. "The temperature is dropping, and a gale is starting to blow snow. And fast!"

Johnny joined Wheeler in the barn distributing oats among Becky Sharp, Black, Buck, Fan, and General Grant. Becky Sharp was far superior in gait than her horse and cart partner Fan. Scarcely keeping her feet on the ground when towing; she ran like a racehorse when Johnny rode her bareback. Bending down to gather a handful of hay, General Grant stealthily took off Johnny's cap. He was a smart and handsome stallion normally into mischief, and a perfect scamp. Each time Johnny overlooked placement of his mittens or clothing articles, General Grant carried them off in a flash.

With chores done, Wheeler and Johnny hurried to the door. The length of time spent in the barn caring for the horses and few cows and pigs, now chilled both man and boy to the bone. Each never knew such cold here. Making their way out of the barn, a violent blow hit, surrounding them in white. Wheeler hollered deafened words to Johnny. Though the man was holding tight to the boy's hand, his words became lost in the piercing roar of the wind. The house, a mere thirty yards away, was veiled by the blizzard [the term blizzard was coined just three years earlier in print on April 23, 1870 by an Estherville, Iowa reporter working for the *Northern Vindicator* newspaper.] For every step forward the pair took, gale force winds blew them ten steps backward underfoot of the crystalline snow. Taking in oxygen became strenuous as fast moving air created pressure, like a vacuum, too strong for chest muscles to exhale expired air from their lungs properly. The twosome became disoriented and lost.

A break in the roar of the wind came for only a few seconds. Johnny and Wheeler heard Jyp, the Mildrums dog, barking wildly from inside the house. The pair, only a few short steps away from the house, had no idea they were that close. Orrin made it home before the brunt of the storm hit, and moments before Johnny and Wheeler staggered through the front door.

On the 9th, the storm was subsiding, but still unstable. Wheeler forced the horses against the wind collecting Julia at the Wells residence. By Friday, January 10th, the prairies were bare, aside from snow drifts up to twenty feet deep along the bluffs. The severity of the 1873 blizzard impacting Minnesota, Iowa and bordering states [the Mildrums lived twelve miles from the Minnesota boarder] took nearly three hundred lives, and consumed thousands of animals and wildlife.

Storm reports from numerous cities filtered in to every major newspaper across the country. On Wednesday, January 8th, the snow was piled so high on the Davenport and St Paul Railroad line near Delaware Center, Iowa, teams of horses were driven over the cars, with drifts stretching three thousand feet long and fifteen feet deep. In Blue Earth, Minnesota, inhabitants could pass on foot over telegraph wires. People were frozen within a stone's throw of their own doors, and were lost. A little girl, living twenty miles from the Mildrums froze her hands and feet so badly, amputation was necessary. The girl's father and mother froze to death. In Sioux City a man and his thirteen year old son left their house on Tuesday for a load of wood. On Friday they were found frozen to death eighty yards apart. The boys' arms were crossed as if he had tried to keep his buttonless overcoat closed. The lad's faithful dog was found alive lying beside him. Seven school children froze to death at Fort Ridgely in Minnesota. The schoolmistress discharged her scholars telling them to "run home quickly." Some of the children made it home, but seven became lost due to the blinding wind and snow. Two sisters were found frozen to death in each others arms; tears of ice affixed to their innocent cheeks. Twenty-four people died at Sleepy Eye Lake, and a New Ulm, Minnesota undertaker made ready twenty caskets a day. School teacher, Hugh Jones, near New Ulm kept forty of his scholars in the schoolhouse from Tuesday until Friday risking his own life trudging daily through two mile drifts to get food for the students. Later, one of the drifts in which the teacher passed was found a man frozen to death while sitting on the seat of his sleigh. His head was buried five feet under the snowy surface. A couple just married were on their way home to Lemars, Iowa when the storm overtook them. They turned the horses loose and overturned the sleigh, then crawled under it wrapping themselves in buffalo robes. The couple remained there for two days and two nights, and when finally rescued were found alive.

The Great Storm of 1873 brought attention to the urgent need of signal stations for the observation of weather over the Northwest, and a more complete connection with the Canadian Weather Bureau. The fearful snow storm which turned Minnesota and Iowa into a polar region reminiscent of a glacial epoch came from Canada. "If suitable signal stations were spread throughout the country, people might be better prepared for inclement weather changes by way of magnetic telegraph and marine signals," urged newspapers. Canada's Signal Corps and America's Signal Station located in Washington merely began three years prior to the storm of 1873.

Seasonal change transpired, and wheat harvest always came in the hottest and driest part of the summer, and was considered the hardest work of the year. The farmers helped each other with the harvesting of the crops. One farmer owned a thresher [separating grain from a plant] and the other farmers would help him harvest his crop. In return he would bring his threshing machine to their farms. They then went from one farm to the other until all of the grain was harvested. Threshing day also meant cooking all day over a hot kitchen stove for the women feeding hungry men that toiled from dawn to sunset.

Due to failing health, Orrin retained a reaping crew to cut and bind the sheaves of grain into shocks in the time honored –way of heads up; stalks to the ground leaning together. This allowed the grain to mature and dry in the field before transport of the grain into the separator of the thresher, but heavy rains damped down any chance of obtaining number one premium quality wheat. At this time, the price of wheat at market brought in $.75 per bushel, and Orrin was hopeful his crop of oats and barley would improve.

The day dawned bright and early as the harvesters pulled into the field ready to devour amber waves of grain fluttering in the warm August breeze. Johnny was excited watching the wheat field take on a whirl of bent backed men beneath the vivid sunlight, threshing, grabbing, lifting, pitching and tossing. The crew operated a fixed steam engine operating the threshing machine, while stacked bundles scattered over the field were carried in by men with chapped raw hands to a mechanized thresher knocking wheat kernels off the dried plants cleaning the grain. Johnny was in charge of hitching the team [of horses] to pull the steam engine from place to place in the field, and helped muscled men pitch fork straw from piles giving rise to tumultuous squalls of chaff bracts. Stalks of grain fed into the mouth of the thresher by men, sustained belts and pulleys advancing the load to a cylinder beating the grain from the stalks. Detached kernels filled the machine's belly at the same time exiting straw out the back. The grain would be stored for later use of ground flour, market delivery on the road to Cresco, or saved as seed wheat for the following year.

One of the workers on the crew was a nomadic fellow the field boss called, "Little Bill." Julia would have called him a tramp. She kept an unpracticed loaded revolver behind her pantry door for reasons of light-fingered incidents prevalent in the area. Recently, farmer owned chickens, hides, hay and grain, along with horses, horse blankets, and harnesses were missing, but "Little Bill" was a first-rate worker. As the thresher slowly began to fail, Bill jumped upon the feed board to ascertain the situation. There appeared a belt needing adjustment on the engine driving the machine. Bill reached his arm across exposed moving parts, when an edge of his long sleeved hickory shirt caught. Standing nearby, Johnny caught sight as Bill's shirt disappeared from his back like Houdini. He rapidly stopped the machine before the upper limbs and torso of the man turned into something catastrophic. Bill stood agape pinching a scrap of cloth between two fingers.

Johnny dismissed any notion of heroism when Julia delivered lunch. The men told her if it hadn't been for Johnny, "Little Bill may now be severely mutilated." They all needed the break. A cool gray jug passed by each man grasping and swinging it high enough to guzzle a considerable amount of thirst quenching water. Milk, cheese, bread, spare ribs, and fried cakes curbed their hunger, and afterward they all rested. Johnny laid back into the straw stack veiling the fiery hot sun with a straw hat shading his face. Soon dubious thoughts of what might have happened to Bill were replaced with katydids chirping and crackling. Buzzing wings of flies annoyed the horses amid the stirring winds of rustling wheat, when the crew boss shouted, "time to roll out!"

⚜

Christmas came early that year. A postal arrived in the direction of Orrin and Julia by way of the Express Company that a barrel awaited pick up at the Osage station twenty miles away. The ride along the Cedar Valley railroad which runs through Central Iowa and crosses the Mississippi at Dubuque would make for a much longer route than via the Milwaukee and St. Paul railroad. Johnny turned the horned animals and the colts loose in the field, gave the porkers heaps of corn, and gallons of porridge, then tied Buck to the fence with a loaf of bread and pail of slops by his side to keep him company. As the trio set out in the direction of Riceville inside a lumber wagon, Buck came capering along after them. Johnny went back and tied the horse repeatedly. Julia was certain that when going back several times before starting a journey insured the family good luck. By the time they reached Riceville, water came above the hubs, causing Becky and Fan to loose footing along a slippery bank where a new bridge was under construction. However, the team pulled them through the quagmire securing a safe trip. Once home, Julia declared, "I've ridden in a lumber wagon for ten years, and now I want a wagon with springs!"

Julia made a warming winter supper of prairie chicken [grouse genus,] and partridge [pheasant species,] her favorite. Johnny was not as particular to quality, as he was about quantity, and feasted on apples and plums, abundant this year, as the threesome gathered around the table taking in the warmth of an open fire until bellies were full.

Orrin commenced opening the barrel with hammer and chisel, as Johnny talked incessantly unable to control his excitement.

"Who sent it? What's in it? Can I see?" The barrel's contents held books, *Pennsylvania Pilgrim, and Snow Bound*, written by poet John Greenleaf Whittier, and *Recollections of Seventy Years*, by Mrs. John Farrar, [from Kittie Skerry, friend and former Granville, MA. Seminary classmate.] Orrin's sister-in-law included soap and Helen [Julia's sister] sent Johnny a framed picture of the entire North family. Layer after layer inside the barrel contained articles. A boiled shirt [a formal or semiformal dress shirt with a starched front,] flannel shirts, buttoned night shirts, overcoats, overshoes, and caps for Johnny and Orrin. Paper, envelopes, sixteen 3 cent postage stamps came next. Orrin's family sent him a fomenter, which he promptly filled with hot water and laid it to the left of his aching diaphragm. Julia tugged from the barrel a calico dress, skirt, chemiloons [a garment for women consisting of chemise and drawers united into one,] and a box of hair pins. She delighted in the slim cut of the dress dancing about with her new dress as her partner as lambent light of early evening fell through the kitchen window. "I won't have to wear hoops with this one, or get my heels caught in them," she joyfully caroled.

Arranged underneath the softness of a buffalo robe, rested a nut cracker and a sack of hickory nuts. Scarves, buttons and an album came next inside the container. Selected after that were newspapers, handkerchiefs, oil stone, tools, socks and stockings, chocolate, sheet songs, and catalogues. A foot mat made of brilliant woven material, not the braided corn husk mats Julia laced in her home, came next. At the bottom of the barrel, arranged in neat stacks of bow tied ribbon, rested several treasured letters from home. Johnny thought it the best Thanksgiving he ever had, and Orrin later surprised him with a magnificently carved wooden sled.

VIII

"Mr. Mildrum bought an acre of land, and started a
hardware store and tin shop in Riceville, finally moving
off the farm and into town where he had built a store
and dwelling combined. Soon he was taken with
consumption [pulmonary tuberculosis] and died
suddenly. Mrs. Mildrum had just returned from visiting
her family in the East before he passed away."

–Johnny

The family moved seven miles down the road to Riceville, which lay in parts of Mitchell and Howard Counties, served by the Chicago Great Western Railway. On the Mitchell County side of the line several groceries and dry goods stores dotted Main Street, with shoe and drug stores sandwiched in-between. At the far end of the counties' dividing line [Main Street known as Woodland Avenue] a flour mill, blacksmith shop, and creamery stood. The Howard County side boasted hotels, a feed mill, and Mildrum's Hardware store. Arthur Noble, Orrin's nephew from Cromwell, Connecticut settled in as tinsmith of the business anchoring a big shears in a hole of a work bench, a hand snips and nippers for cutting, straight and curved anvils for turning and rolling the edges of the tin, and a soldering iron and fire pot to join wire and flattened tinplate together.

He had adopted the tinsmith trade from his father, and agreed to manage the business due to Orrin's deteriorating health.

From 1869 until 1883, there were no direct rail connections into Riceville, and mail was brought from Osage by stage coach. Letters connected migrants with the homes they had left behind, and helped to build an interconnecting network of people across the vast new country that was developing. News from home, news from the frontier, news from the city—all of these things traveled by post, and letters became the tie that bound together a disparate and radically changing country. Many Americans saw the newly acquired territories in the West as an opportunity to start a new life. Letters of this kind were all too common on the frontier, where the death rate was high and the possibility of news traveling by any other route remote.

Because letters were the sole means of communication for Americans who moved westward during the early nineteenth century, letters had the power both to warm the heart with good news and to break it with bad.

> "Orrin is sick again with Rheumatic attacks. He has taken Colchicum (for gout) by the gallon and Sulphur (for gout and rheumatism) by the bushels, and Sarsaparilla (for inflammation) by the bottle. He is much blistered with mustard from his neck to his hips, and par broiled with hot applications and skinned with liniments, all to no purpose. The worst place seems to be in the left region of the short ribs though it goes to the right side and up and down each side of the spinal column. Dreadful cramps seem to come from his diaphragm. I have used hot salt and water applications, and today am applying wet flannels of hot vinegar in which red peppers have been boiled. I haven't been using both things freely for fear of driving the Rheumatism to his heart. Our physician said he can do nothing more for him.

Pneumonia and Lung Fever seem to be quite common here. [Pneumonia is an inflammation of one or both lungs, in which the air sacs become filled with liquid, which renders them useless for breathing. It is usually caused by bacterial or viral infection. The condition in the nineteenth century was often called Lung Fever.] Will you send more sugar pills? [In homeopathy, diluted substances are considered to have a higher potency and a deeper-acting remedy resulting as indistinguishable from the dilutants of sugar, alcohol and water.] I should not apply to you if I knew of anyone who is not a quack Homeopathic in this region. Johnny has been sick, missing several days of school.

Schuyler Colfax, past vice-president with Ulysses S. Grant, is to speak in Osage the day after tomorrow. I was going to attend the lecture with our friends in Stacyville, Fitch and Amy (Sewall) Stacy, but their little boy Ralph has Spiralis Meningitis [the condition in the early nineteenth century was also labeled Brain Fever.] He has a high fever, severe headache, and stiff neck. I am healthy, and my hundred and sixty pounds speak well of it. Many children have Whooping Cough [deaths from whooping cough remained in the region of 10,000 a year from 1847 until the 1900s.]

I am sorry to hear of the prevalence of Typhoid Fever among you. The Dr. told me a few days ago that there was considerable of it about here usually combined with Bilious, and he considers it very dangerous. [Typhoid Fever is an infectious, often fatal, feverish disease, characterized by intestinal inflammation and ulceration caused by the bacterium Salmonella typhi living only in humans. Persons with typhoid fever carry the bacteria in their bloodstream and intestinal tract. Both ill persons and carriers shed *Salmonella* Typhi in their feces (stool). The name came from the disease's similarity to Typhus. Other terms used for typhoid fever in the early nineteenth century were Enteric Fever, Slow Fever, Nervous Fever, and Long Fever. Biliousness is a complex of symptoms comprising nausea, abdominal discomfort, headache, and constipation so as to include excessive secretion of bile from the liver. The condition was also known as Intermittent Fever.]"

– Jule

Highly contagious diseases—cholera, smallpox, diphtheria and typhoid fever—spread quickly from person to person. Typhus, an infectious disease caused by several micro-organism species of Rickettsia (transmitted by lice and fleas) and characterized by exhaustion and weakness, high fever, depression, delirium, headache, and a peculiar eruption of reddish spots on the body. The epidemic or classic form is louse borne; the endemic form is flea borne. Other names used for Typhus Fever include Malignant Fever (used in the 1850s), Jail Fever, Hospital Fever, Ship Fever, Putrid Fever, Brain Fever, Bilious Fever, Spotted Fever, Petechial Fever, and Camp Fever. Iowa established a State Board of Health in 1880.

Early settlers did not have the use of antibiotics. The search for antibiotics began in the late 1800s with the growing acceptance of the germ theory for disease. As a result, scientists began to devote time in searching for drugs that would kill disease causing bacteria. Penicillin wasn't invented until 1928, but not until March 14, 1943, a moldy cantaloupe in a Peoria, Illinois market was found to contain the best and highest quality penicillin after a worldwide search. The discovery of the cantaloupe, and the results of fermentation research on corn steep liquor at the Northern Regional Research Laboratory at Peoria, allowed the United States to produce 2.3 million doses in time for the invasion of Normandy in the spring of 1944.

Orrin Mildrum, born October 26, 1829 in Middletown,

Connecticut, died September 30, 1878, in Riceville, Iowa. Dr. Walker concluded that a hay seed previously lodged in Orrin's lungs was the source of his lung infection. Consumption or Tuberculosis (TB) [also known as Phthisis and Marasmus] is a potentially fatal contagious disease that can affect almost any part of the body, but is mainly an infection of the lungs caused by a bacterial microorganism, the *tubercle bacillus* or *Mycobacterium tuberculosis*. Few diseases have caused so much distressing illness for centuries and claimed so many lives. Forty-nine-year-old Orrin Mildrum was laid to rest in Riverside Cemetery in Riceville, Iowa. Walking from the cemetery adrift in emotion, the seeds of discord began to grow in Johnny. He felt lost and unsure, feeling confused and frustrated. An ache barricaded his heart, but he could not explain it. He did not know how to release the anguish he was feeling. Then his shoulders shook as he cried for every last repressed emotion. He cried for an angry and confused heart. He cried for the loneliness, the pain, and the ache he felt during his childhood. The burdens began to lessen their toll on his exhausted body with each sob, until he let go of all the pain. Johnny softly whispered, "Thank you for wanting--- me."

⚜

> *"I always loved band music. Anytime a band came*
> *to Riceville, I was the first one there if possible.*
> *Rob Noble had an old cornet, and he let me blow it.*
> *Before long I could play several tunes."*
>
> *– Johnny*

On a stopover to California, Rob Noble [Arthur's brother,] came for a visit. One day he appeared at the store with a shiny brass cornet. "Here," he said to Johnny, "learn to play this. It's a wind instrument.

Johnny took the instrument. It was beautiful. It felt perfect in his hands. It just felt right.

"Well, give it a try, and see what you think," Rob declared with a light-hearted spirit.

Johnny opened his lips and blew. A gush of warm saliva filled the mouthpiece, producing an unpleasant wet sound. Arthur took hold, released the spit, and then handed it back. "Dampen your lips first, then place the tip of your tongue between them, like this," Rob demonstrated the facial change. "Now tighten the corners of your lips and flatten your chin. At once pull your tongue back slightly until it clears the lips. You want to leave a slight opening between the lips to blow the air out. You need air to vibrate those lips, Johnny. You got to push the sound through."

Johnny did as told, and a much better, yet weak sound came through the horn.

"Use your diaphragm, John. Pull air into it so you have the strength to push out the notes," Arthur urged, giving the impression of a puffed-out rooster controlling his roost.

From that day foreword, Johnny spent every free minute practicing the cornet. He listened to the sounds around him—from the hoot owls hunkering in the shadows of natural timber, to the sounds of Beaver Creek washing over fringes of woodland, to the music of songbirds and their symphonies of spontaneous melody—absorbing it all as inspiration. He learned to modify the air column's vibration by changing lip aperture. He discovered that using one or more valves on the piece of equipment changed the length of vibration and pitch. He learned that music helped him release pent up emotions and handle his frustrations. Johnny proved to be a quick study, and on no account was deficient of a cornet in his hands again. Before long he exhibited remarkable talent. His grades in school improved, and Orrin and Julia were proud of him.

Around the age of sixteen, Johnny enrolled in Cedar Valley Seminary for two terms. Osage, the judicial seat of Mitchell County in the heart of the Cedar Valley river, along the Cedar Falls and Minnesota and the Illinois Central Railroad, and eighteen miles east of Riceville, held a college for moral, mental, and useful training of mind— Cedar Valley Seminary.

At this school, study selections went according to special needs. The teacher's course, requiring one, two, or three years study, according to the advancement of the student, was designed to fit students for a higher position in the teaching profession. The business courses were arranged for those who wanted to devote two or three terms chiefly to penmanship, business arithmetic, bookkeeping, and commercial law. The scientific courses, of four years, included all the leading sciences and a full course in history, English literature, and the German language. The literary course gave way to three years of the Latin language and literature. The classics course yielded a year and a half in Greek in place of science and other literary studies, and the music courses engaged instruction of instrumental and vocal music and harmony. Johnny studied music for two terms. He learned the balance between playing by ear and reading notes to play an instrument. "Visualize the chords and scales," Mr. Eaton instructed. And soon Johnny gained the ability to read and play notes, ranking top in this class. One evening, after a rave performance for the school's Vaudeville Night, Johnny was invited to join the Osage Cornet Band.

❧

In nearly every brass band, there is usually only one E ♭ cornet pitched a fourth above the standard B. A soprano E ♭ cornet adds an extreme high register to the brass band sound, effectively cutting through even the loudest *tutti* (all orchestra), and Johnny played the E ♭ in the Osage Band. His lips gained control over the wind instrument, emanating a warm, mellow tone, distinguishing it from the penetrating sound of the trumpet. "Hey, you're really good on that thing," complimented one band member, "you should think about hooking up with the Sixth Regiment." Before long Johnny quit school and joined the Iowa State's Militia, advancing as a member of the redesigned National Guard Sixth Regiment band and escaping the Spanish American War when the band followed the regiment, going off to war with instruments cased and rifles over their shoulders. Johnny continued as a band member, until he needed money.

That year, Johnny hired out for fifty dollars, with board and washing, on the farm of Treasurer, Ed Shipard of Osage in Mitchell County, before moving onto a tinner's trade. Johnny knew something of the craft from attention paid helping Orrin, but after six months of working for Herman Miniger, a New York inhabitant of Osage, Johnny made the transition to Ashland, Wisconsin, to work for the Davis Tinsmith Shop.

While in Ashland, Johnny joined the City Band, and came in contact with two fine band directors, Harry Hap and JJ Cross. Professor Cross, a refined cornet soloist, singled out Johnny. "Hey, you can really slot in and out of solos and bridges." Johnny felt proud to receive such high praise from one as admirable as JJ Cross. The Italian gained an abundance of musical education from both men, and the cornet bedded Johnny's American Dream. He could do most anything with this brilliant brass instrument, and like a transient, Johnny found himself back in Osage working in a tin shop and performing odd jobs.

Johnny helped at the hardware store and worked for native New Yorker, Captain Charles Fitch Gardner. The captain was the father of band member and friend, William Gardner. Johnny and William's friendship began as members of the Sixth Regiment Band, and later grew to playing several required instruments in the Happy Hooligan Band. William was known as Happy. "We can sure use the help," alleged William one night after a gig. "The ever-bearing strawberry market is doing well." At an early age the captain had begun assisting his father, Nathaniel, in the work of the fields, and so had become thoroughly familiar with the best methods of tilling the soil and caring for the crops. Soon the Gardner's owned ten acres in Howard County, into which Gardner's Nursery launched and grew in the Mississippi Valley. The captain began experimenting with the ever-bearing strawberry, promoting several varieties of exceptional size and quality that bore fruit from the middle of July until the middle of October, when frost freezes the plant. In addition to mail order sales, a preserving factory was established, canning more than one thousand quarts per day of the ever-bearing fruit for large quantity sales. The captain propagated plums, was the originator of the ever berry strawberry, and Oriental poppies. He crossed the English walnut with the butternut with great success. Immense beds of asparagus, great vineyards where many kinds of grapes were cultivated, fruit trees of all kinds, all varieties of berry nursery stock, flowers, and hardy shrubs loomed across the acreage. No one could speculate that in later years William's daughter [Grace] would one day marry Johnny's son [Linton.]

❧

The hardware business continued with Arthur as sole proprietor, affording a successful business, and Julia slacked off of her business duties in defense of free time. One day as Julia paged through a seed   catalogue, she saw an advertisement for everlasting grass.

"Look! Perpetual green grass seed," she said with a reformer's zeal. "This would be so nice for Orrin's burial site," showing the listing to Arthur. "Imagine, an everlasting carpet of green grass," she sighed. "Orrin would be so pleased to know he's resting in green pastures. I believe I'd like to order some." When the seed arrived, Julia seeded down the grave, and before long the everlasting grass grew. It grew so fast that it was soon out of hand, spreading throughout the cemetery, reaching Kellow's farm, and making its way toward Mill Pond. "For God's sake Aunt Jule, you're no better than Typhoid Mary," Arthur quipped as the two stood among overgrown vegetation. "You planted quack grass!"

IX

*"In my teens, I got the job of teacher of the Riceville
Cornet band. For the little I knew, the band members were
determined. They worked hard and did well. Later
I was called to Le Roy, Minnesota to put a band in order.
For the next two years, I organized additional bands
in Elma and Lime Springs, Iowa, and while in
Lime Springs met Sophie Jane Hughes.*

*In 1889 I joined Boston's Uncle Tom's Cabin show in
Brookings, South Dakota, and stayed with the group until
tent season closed, then I followed Fitzpatrick's Rip Van
Winkle show. I learned a great deal from Fritz Töniges,
the leader of the show band and orchestra, and a very fine
musician from Germany. We traveled for awhile through
the southern states, before making our way north to
Indiana, Michigan and eastern Wisconsin.*

*In June of 1890 I left the show and returned to Riceville,
Le Roy and Osage. That fall I was called to Superior,
Wisconsin taking charge of the Superior City band until
August. Two weeks before departure, I performed with and
directed a circus band for the Great Western Shows
in Superior, Wisconsin and Duluth, Minnesota."*

–Johnny

At long last, in the spring of 1882, Julia left Iowa. Moving East to live with sisters Harriet [Dowd and family] and Helen [North] in Saratoga Springs, New York, Julia continued to teach and enlisted herself as bookkeeper at Temple Grove Ladies Seminary. Arthur and Rob Noble [Orrin's nephews] took over the store entirely as Noble's Hardware store. Without hesitation, seventeen-year-old Johnny stayed in Iowa. Music was his life, and he groomed himself as a self sufficient musician.

Riceville organized a cornet band. The band struck up one of those over and over strains that seemed to have no beginning and certainly no ending—moaning wails like a presiding elder preaching at a revival meeting. Otis Woodard, a band member from Osage begged Johnny to instruct the band in composition. "You're a natural, John, and already a member. The guys will learn a great deal from you. You've got to take it!" So, Johnny took on the job of teacher, becoming a professor of music in his teens. He gave private lessons, demonstrated to his tutorial groups the purity of tone in which he played, and imparted what he could of his gift for improvisation. "We're not signaling orders on a battlefield. Without valves, your instrument is nothing more than a bugle. The valves change the length of the vibrating column, resulting in melodic passages, not the piercing notes of a trumpet," he explained to his protégé's.

❧

At the age of twenty-one, Johnny became a citizen of the United States of America on October 5, 1886 in the Mitchell County district courthouse in Osage. Johnny experienced mixed emotion of happiness and sadness that day. Poignant reflections of early childhood brought to mind burning questions. *"Why didn't my parents come look for me? Did they love me? Why did they hand me off to the*

padroni? Were they so desperate for money to sell their own child?"
But, America took him in and gave him a new life. The Mildrum's
gave him God, security, an education, and love. Johnny's passion for
music encouraged him to look for new ways to grow and improve;
his mindset striving toward a positive attitude. Early on, he'd recognized the arrival of uninvited thoughts and emotions. He dealt
with his feelings accordingly and recognized decisive happiness
made him feel happy, and pessimism sad. He learned to let go and
forgiveness set Johnny free.

The immigration officers congratulated him on becoming
a new US citizen, and Johnny departed the building embraced in a
personal triumph of self worth.

⁂

For the next two years Johnny played cornet in bands and or-
chestras of traveling troupe's. Music became something bigger than
Johnny himself while touring the country as a professional musician
in *Uncle Tom's Cabin*. He absorbed music theory and music history
gaining further knowledge from the masters of music branching out
as an eminent virtuoso.

Harriet Beecher Stowe's 1852 anti-slavery novel, *Uncle Tom's
Cabin*; or, *Life Among the Lowly,* took on the theme of the immorality of slavery by means of community adapted minstrels, plays, and
musicals at the turn of the 19th century. More than four hundred
separate companies traveled and presented the *Tom Shows*, as they
were known, for nearly ninety years in opera houses, theaters, halls,
barns, tents and showboats. Those were the days of oil lamps. If the
janitor walked from the wings to the center of the stage to trim a
flickering wick during a scene, nothing was thought of it.

When the *Tom Shows* came to town, bands often strutted into the streets in pompous glory bellowing minor chords full of music with their instruments leading the company of *Uncle Tom's Cabin*, while eager crowd's pressed forward into the street as the band strutted by. In addition to the parade, brass bands performed, and blackface [makeup applied to a performer playing a black person in a minstrel show] performers.

Many minstrel shows faithfully reflected Stowe's sentimentalized antislavery politics of evil and immorality, while others plays varied moderately to pro-slavery attacks on an established way of life. In either case, the impact of Stowe's book, *Uncle Tom's Cabin,* is deemed to have served as a spark to light the fuse of the powder keg of the War Between the States [Civil War.] Ms. Stowe's book is a landmark of American literature.

Uncle Tom's Cabin was not the first book to inspire advertising, other traveling shows brought about Washington Irving's 1819 reserve, *Rip Van Winkle*, for theaters, vaudeville and opera houses. Irving's book dealt with political issues, the American Revolution, and comical gender issues involving a lazy husband and a bad-tempered wife.

❧

Riceville, Iowa-- A man will arrive in town next week with a carload of children, which he will peddle out to those that feel disposed to give a home to the homeless.

Elma, Iowa--Professor J.M. Arsers, our band instructor, tells us that while he was in Riceville last week he met Mr. E. Trott, who came from New York with a band of orphans and waifs for whom he was seeking homes. Twenty-five years ago the same gentleman helped bring Mr. Arsers out along with a number of other children for whom he found homes in the

west. Professor Arsers still cherishes a kindly feeling toward
that gentleman owing to the kind mission in which he is
engaged.

–Osage, Iowa News, Oct. 14, 1897

In October 1897, on a weekly trip into Riceville to teach music, Johnny met the man who once rescued him off the streets of New York. Standing on a platform of the newly built depot of the Chicago Great Western Railroad stood Eli Trott. Johnny recognized the tall suited man immediately. His hair now thin and grey, the man's face took on an air of serenity, one in which Johnny remembered long ago.

"Forgive me sir, but are you Mr. Trott from the Children's Aid Society?" Johnny asked approaching the man surrounded by a group of children.

"Yes, that's right. Are you here to select a child from the train? There are many needing a good home, but I'm afraid this group has been claimed," replied the elderly gent.

"I once stood in those children's very shoes," Johnny responded with a grin.

"Jean (*Zhahn*) is it you? I scarcely forget a child's face. Still, I see far off Italy in your brown eyes. What have you done with your life, Jean (*Zhahn*)? Tell me!"

Johnny gave his former caregiver a quick rundown of his life, and by the time he finished, Mr. Trott was bursting with pride patting Johnny on the back while suppressing a hint of moisture in his eyes.

"Children, attention please," Mr. Trott broadcast. "I want you to meet someone. This is John. He was once just like you, and got off an orphan train not far from here. He, my dear boy's and girl's, is a prime example of what hard work and study can do for you. Mr.

Arsers is now a music professor and a leader of several brass bands as a business. John, do you have anything you'd like to say to the children?"

Johnny was caught off guard. He thought for a minute, and then said, "Always believe in yourself, and dream big! No one can ever take your dreams away from you, because you own them. Keep what's important sorted out, and make good choices. I made plenty of mistakes, but I learned from them to become a better person. I tell my music students to focus on one pitch at a time, and eventually there is great improvement."

The children were encouraged. Questions came forth like weeds in neglected soil. "Did ye learnt ta play da music yerself? Did yea git good folks? Did you ever run away? What if our new folks don't treat us right? *Was u bang*? (Were you afraid? Spoken by a young boy the children called Dutch.)"

"It all happened so fast. I was given a triangle to play in the streets of France." At the mention of her mother country, one French (François) girl timidly smiled. "The people that took me in, here, were good people. Both of them believed study and school important. I got lucky there. I thought about running away, especially when things got hard for me, like learning the English language, doing chores and working hard in the fields. But my folks never gave up on me. Should any of you meet with ill treatment, tell someone you trust. Keeping asking until you find someone who will listen to you."

Mr. Trott announced enough time had been taken, and Johnny needed to attend business. The men shook hands and hugged before parting company. As Johnny made himself ready to leave the depot, a boy, around the age of nine, tugged on his coat sleeve in need of speaking. Groping for the right English words, but with the Italian words balanced on the edge of his tongue, the English words became lost. "Posso essere il tuo bambino! (I can be your child!)"

the boy exclaimed.

Mamma mia! (My goodness!) Dove sono i genitori che hanno scelto tu? (Where are the parents who have chosen you?) The lad pointed to a man and woman waiting near a buggy, and told Johnny this was his second trip west this year. The previous family had worked him harder than a horse in the fields, from sun up to sun down, that the adolescent collapsed under the strain. Johnny took the boy's hand and walked with him to the buggy. After talking with the couple, Johnny looked in the direction of the boy and said, "Brava gente," (good people.) A worried look quickly vanished from the boy's brave face. Cheerfully smiling, he waved good-bye toward Johnny.

By the time the relocation program ended [1929] youngsters were scattered across the breadth of America.

✌

While in Osage, Johnny took up with the Sixth Regiment band, and taught and organized bands in Le Roy, and Winona [Minnesota,] and in Stacyville and Bailey [Iowa.] Johnny married Sophie Hughes, (in 1891) and started a family of his own before moving on to St. Ansgar [Iowa.] (Over time the couple would take pleasure in raising seven children.)

> St. Ansgar Enterprise, Oct. 19, 1898--- Professor Arsers came home from a trip last Friday evening on the Clipper [train]. The professor is in demand in a good many places as a band instructor and he gives instruction every evening in the week. He is at Riceville Tuesday evening, at Elma Wednesday evening, at Alta Vista Thursday evening, and at Osage Friday evening. St. Ansgar alone is fortunate enough to have his services two evenings in the week, and of course that is a guarantee that we will have a better band than any of the other places.

Stacyville, Iowa Band 1880. John Arsers, third from left holding cornet.

Sixth Regiment Band, 1880s. Back row, fifth from left, John Arsers.

St Ansgar, Iowa Band, 1890s. Back row, third from left, John Arsers.

Riceville, Iowa Band early 1900s. Kneeling right, John Arsers.

X

"In the spring of 1901, I got a call from Park Rapids,
Minnesota through an old friend, Everett Page,
[a former Jamestown neighbor] who had played with me
in the Riceville band. I packed up my family, and
we moved there in May. We lived in Park Rapids
four years, and had a very good band.

That spring we moved to Akeley, Minnesota where
I conducted a furniture and secondhand store.
had a similar store in Park Rapids and took some stock
from there leaving the Park Rapids store in charge of my
brother-in-law, George Hughes [the Hughes family,
with the exception of Sophie's father, Henry, of Rome,
New York, settled in Lime Springs, Iowa]."

–Johnny

Johnny and his family escaped the 1901 Riceville, Iowa fire. On July 20, 1901, Riceville was an active community and hub of local business. The day was very hot (104 degrees), and the weather had been hot and dry for weeks. Around noon, a resident spotted flames coming from the roof of the meat market. In a few hours the fire spread, destroying nearly fifty businesses and twenty homes in the city of Riceville. The total loss reached $200,000, with $100,000 insurance. No lives were lost, but more than twenty families were rendered homeless.

Riceville in Ashes

Riceville, Iowa a town of 1,000 inhabitants on the Chicago Great Western railroad, forty miles south of Hayfield, was visited by a disastrous fire last Saturday afternoon, which consumed between sixty and seventy buildings. The fire was discovered at 12:30 in the back of Cooper's meat market, says the proprietor, where he was frying out lard. It is supposed that some of the hot lard spilled on the floor, became ignited and started the fire, which spread eastward, consuming all before it.

The day was excessively warm, a hot wind from the southwest adding to the fires fearful heat and making conditions in the burning district frightful in the extreme. Scores of people, overcome by the heat, lay in the streets like drunkards. The town has no fire protection, and help was called from neighboring towns. Hundreds came from Elma and Alta Vista on a special run at a rate of over a mile a minute. [Horses drawn engines were used for propulsion, conserving steam pressure for the pumper.] The people worked heroically to save their homes, their places of business and stocks of goods, but the hungry flames leaped from building to building and from street to street, until the entire business portion of the town was in ashes.

Two general stores and one bank remain. The following is a list of places burned:

Congregational and M.E. Churches (and parsonages)
Three hotels
Two drug stores
Three hardware stores
[one of which was Mildrum & Noble hardware store]

One bank

One printing office (Riceville Recorder)

Chicago Great Western depot

Opera house

Post Office

Seven general stores

Two butcher shops

Three milliner shops

One lumber yard

Two blacksmith shops

One dentist office

One law office

One photography gallery

Telephone office

Residences, barns and outbuilding

–July 25, 1901, Dodge County News
Hayfield, Minnesota

Everyone in Riceville initiated an orderly clean-up in the fire's aftermath. Rob and Arthur Noble operated their hardware business along with several Riceville establishments from a make shift community building until rebuilding began in earnest, this time with modern and permanent stores and public buildings. Soon the R.M. Noble Hardware [Robert Mildrum Noble] store was rebuilt and ready for business as usual. [The store flourished until it was sold in 1919. Robert's wife, Cordelia Adams Noble died, and Robert's only daughter, Dollie, accommodated her aging father until he died in 1924. Arthur moved on to the state of Oregon with his wife and daughter where he died in 1915.]

Returning to Iowa in 1911, Johnny continued as conductor and director of bands in Osage, Riceville, Le Roy, Elma, Alta Vista, McIntire, Little Cedar, Orchard, St. Ansgar, Lyle, Floyd, Stacyville,

New Haven, Wykoff, Grand Meadow, Spring Valley, Taopi, Adams, and Chester.

Johnny played in several cornet, brass, concert, jazz, symphonic, and big bands in Minnesota and Iowa. In 1920, as Johnny finished an engagement in Davenport, he heard strains of jazz and blues drifting to the banks of the Mississippi as he walked to the train station. A forceful rhythm met Johnny as he stepped on deck of a docked riverboat carrying King Oliver's Creole Jazz Band. Johnny took a seat in the vessel's far corner as he listened to young lion Louis Armstrong play second cornet with a deep, smoky style. Johnny closed his eyes, allowing his senses to savor the flavors and aromas of a remarkable culinary hub of music—a versatile fusion of ragtime, blues, and jazz—when abruptly a voice startled him. "Someone sitting here?" a young man with a close-cropped mustache and slick wavy hair parted down the middle asked.

"Have a seat. I'm John Arsers," Johnny said, extending his hand.

"Bix. Bix Beiderbecke," the seventeen-year-old reciprocated. "I grew up here in Davenport and heard King Oliver was in town. Wouldn't miss this for anything."

Johnny and Bix talked and learned of each other's similar interests and talents in entertainment. Bix was a self-taught cornet and piano player. He informed Johnny of the enjoyment he gained in listening to several recordings of Nick LaRocca, the leader of the Dixieland Jazz Band. His Victrola phonograph machine played LaRocca's music over and over again, causing deep grooves in the shellac of the 78-RPM discs from the stylus [needle] to bottom out. "Nicky inspires me. Maybe someday I'll name a song "Davenport Blues," remembering tonight," he guffawed as he produced a flask of illegal moonshine. Bix said it wasn't illegal as long as the liquor wasn't sold and existed for medicinal purposes. "Sacramental wine is sold to the religious, you know," he said. So Bix tipped a salute to

Iowa's Bible belt while faking a sore tooth by massaging his jaw as Templeton's rye whiskey ran sweet and smooth down his throat. Johnny rejected Bix's offer of a swig, never having had a drop of liquor before. He knew Iowa provided easy access to a key ingredient for the manufacture of alcohol—corn. He also knew that country bootleggers in the area made moonshine whiskey, wine, gin, and home brew beer in caves, basements, wood lots, and in clandestine underground hog houses and barns. The Eighteenth Amendment of the United States Constitution had established prohibition in the United States, and the Volstead Act had given the Amendment the power to enforce the ban. But Iowa had instituted its own statewide prohibition in 1916, four years before National Prohibition was established.

As the evening wore on, Dixieland music drifted through the air and set in motion uncontrollable forces. People got up and danced in fun and energetic jazz steps. Quick turns, fancy footwork, and long knee slides took on the forms of shuffle and swing, resembling a combination of dance moves of the Charleston, Juba, and Black Bottom. Bix grabbed his instrument beckoning the attention of Louie, as he preferred to be called, and the performer motioned for him to join in on a tune of New Orleans hot jazz. The young men, scarcely five years apart in age, collaborated with their cornets collectively. Impulsively, Johnny, the senior element in the crowd, grabbed his own instrument from its case and chimed in while standing at the table. As the cornets connected, the sounds flourished, each breath rivaling the next, a bastion of notes surpassing physical and emotional pleasure and bringing about huge applause from the assembly.

Afterward the men laughed and talked, and Johnny found common ground with them. Louie had grown up in poverty, had sung in the streets for money, and had been put in an orphanage as a delinquent in the Colored Waif's Home in New Orleans. He'd received musical instruction from the Homes band director and became the leader of the Waif's Home Band, until Joe Oliver took Louie under his wing.

"Papa Joe was my mentor and teacher. I tell ya'll, he could produce a wha-wha buzz, changing the timbre and volume of the cornet like no other," Louie beamed, just thinking of Joe.

"You're not so bad yourself with timbre and inflections," Johnny complimented. "You've got a brilliant and sophisticated technique with an expressive attack, Louie. And that's a gift."

Turning to Bix, he added, "Kid, you're going places with that daring sense of harmony and swing."

Bix grinned, taking delivery of the compliment. "You're pretty good on that cornet, yourself, maestro," said Bix, with Louie nodding in agreement. Only this minute, as his eyes glistened wistfully, Johnny smiled and laughed as if someone had just told him a funny story. He knew he would take everlasting pleasure in remembering this night.

※

Julia Mildrum died January 10, 1923 and buried in Saratoga Springs, New York. She was sixty-two years of age. It was not uncommon for loved ones to become separated from burial grounds, especially when death called in faraway territories. Johnny never made it to her funeral. Instead, putting his hands to his face, he sighed and wept for everyone he'd ever loved.

He was safe and sheltered, and his music evolved and continued to function like a courtship display. He taught, directed, and played in several cornet, brass, concert, jazz, symphonic, and big bands, despite Julia's premature faith in his abilities. Music became

Johnny's shadow and his long good-bye. Note arrangements eased Johnny's intellect up the scale a little at a time, while melodies took him through sad times, gave him jauntiness and energy, created peaceful moments, and impacted his heart. More than seventy years of memories, reminders of his early childhood, growing up, and leaving loved ones behind all became an integral part in Johnny's composition of life.

American Band music emerged as a way of life for the Arsers family, giving strength to the musical genius of Jean *(Zhahn)* Assero. Two of Johnny's sons, Clarence and Earl, carried on the music tradition, playing cornet and becoming nationally recognized. Two grandsons, Bill and Kenny, played the French horn, and the third, Sammy, the cornet. They performed in the United States Navy Band all around the world, billing themselves the "world's finest." After retirement, Bill went on to play among the National Symphony Orchestra in Washington, DC. [Bill is buried behind the tomb of the Unknown Soldier at Arlington National Cemetery.] Named after his grandfather, John Arsers never participated in the Navy band, but played clarinet and sax in many bands, including the Guy DeLeo band [Guy DeLeo came west on an orphan train from the New York Foundling Hospital to the state of Minnesota in 1916] Otto Stock, and the Six Fat Dutchmen, to name a few. Daughters, Lorraine and Clarice, played the flute and clarinet correspondingly.

Dying of a heart attack in a lonely hospital room, John Arsers had lived a life of no regrets. Up until two years prior to his death in Iowa City at the age of seventy-six, [1865-May 18, 1941] Johnny had continued to play, teach, and direct bands. John's epitaph billed him as a celebrated bandmaster of the cornet bands of Iowa, a true friend, fine musician, and a real gentleman.

Johnny

I

SOPHIA'S STORY

The year 1915 was a banner building year for the Bronx, where apartment houses—from the most humble to the most elegant—sprang up. As tenements grew with the rapidity of the first year of a child's life, the Bedford Park section—anchoring immigrant populations of Italian, German, Irish, and Jewish culture—added forty villa sites. The modest neighborhood of Villa Avenue quickly emerged into an Italian sector. In this place, on April 22nd, while a great war raged in her mother country, Italy, which had declared war on Austria-Hungary and Germany, nineteen-year-old Maria gave birth to a child she named Sophia.

Summer gave way to an unpredictable autumn, and on Saturday, October 9th, 1915, weather conditions plummeted toward forty-eight degrees. The Bronx streets were bustling as people went about registering to vote. At the polling places men and women brought each other up to date on the latest news. "Did you hear President Woodrow Wilson, the first president ever to grace his presence at a World Series game, is attending the second game between the Red Sox and the Phillies today?" Or, "Too bad about G.P. Putnam's son of the big publishing firm. Yes, he died of heart failure two days ago. His name was John Bishop, wasn't it, the director of publishing over there in New Rochelle at Knickerbockers Press?"

On Villa Avenue wagons rattled, a door slammed, and a child wailed. A distraught Maria bundled her six-month-old infant in the remnants of a warm blanket as she boarded the Interborough Transit for Manhattan. Her thoughts, adrift, gentle, and vague, coursed like a night breeze, encompassing a circle drawn inside the young woman's mind, and then dwindled to a single point.

In 1914, when Bronx became a County, Maria felt stirring desires for the man who warmed her heart with his soulful smile, the child's father, an attractive German man of Polish nationality. At the time, the compliments he paid her were so generous that she blushed to remember them.

In July, a new terror presented itself. It seemed the rest of Maria's whole life dated from then. She had met him without consciousness and now carried a secret before her. It was beyond her power to put herself aside as she pleaded to the heavens for help. But the heavens were silent, and there came from them no assurance of voice. Storms of thoughts assaulted her as she told her parents that she was pregnant.

Her mother forbid her to see, let alone marry William Kaminsky. After all, he was German-Polish and part of the Jewish people. "Fortunately," she said, "this baby won't be Jewish." Maria was Italian Catholic, and in her mother's eyes, Jewish identity was bestowed on babies of Jewish mothers, and of Jewish mothers and fathers.

Maria thought of William often, and the question of his love rose up before her and demanded a reply as she walked by the place he worked, but he had vanished. Her heart grew less certain, more constrained. A bitter feeling of despair surged. Suddenly a whisper came to her that there was sadly little for her to build upon. She buried her face with her hands as tears gathered in her eyes then slowly trickled down her cheeks, her star of hope gone. William Kaminsky would never know he had a baby girl.

The day was hazy, the air warm and still, vaguely depressing in a season that ought to be brisk. A hint of curly black hair peeked above the dilapidated blanket as Maria revealed her listless six-month-old infant to Mother Jerome, the superior in charge at the New York Foundling Hospital. Close at hand in the waiting chamber was Sister Austin, tapping a well-worn, black lace-up shoe, emphasizing her nervous impatience. Setting her eyes on the infant embraced before her, the nun recognized the child's delicate health needed prompt medical attention. Not able to tolerate the seriousness of the circumstances any longer, instinct set in, and the nun grasped the tiny bundle from Maria's cradled arms, rapidly expressing her intentions. "We must get this child over to the pediatric wing. Dr. Joseph Ohlivyer is in attendance today and will examine her. This child is in grave condition. There is simply no time to waste," the nun admonished.

Escaping with the tiny bundle supported in her arms, Sister Austin quickly made it to the nursery reserved for children with life-threatening illness.

After examination of the ailing infant, Dr. Ohlivyer declared the child's health "POOR," in bold black letters on top of his chart. The physician also noted below the child's name that she was "malnourished," with "strabismus, and languid with enteritis." The doctor thought about all the children he'd formerly seen entering the Foundling dying of identical circumstances. Then he outlined a plan that the infant remain in the nursery until she regained health. Then and only then did he scratch out on paper that the child could be moved to one of the age-appropriate nurseries.

Mother Jerome consoled a worried Maria, "Don't be troubled, my dear. Your child will be well cared for here. She is very sick and must remain in our nursery until she is well. "Are you still breast-feeding her?" Maria answered with an affirmative nod.

"We will make sure she gets plenty of good mother's milk in that case. We outsource many of our infants to wet nurses in the neighborhood, or the women come in to the hospital. These women have recently lost their own child or nurse their own child with one of ours. We have accomplished a much higher infant survival rate by means of this method."

The nun paused to allow Maria to absorb this much, and then went on. "We have always believed it best for a mother and child to remain together, and we strive toward that goal, but often many of our children are products of poor immigrant parents with no means of support."

For months she had fought the world to provide for Sophia. With no husband, and underprivileged parents, the girl struggled to keep her job and take care of an infant. Mother Jerome continued, "Those who are prosperous manage payments to the hospital for their child's care, and some parents are able to recover them. But out of necessity, most ultimately must sacrifice their children for a better chance at life. When the time is right, we place these children in new homes across the country where they will receive love, attention, and healthy lives."

The color left Maria's face, and a chill crept from her limbs into her heart. The young woman threw a withering glace at Mother Jerome as she placed the necessary papers before a pair of clasped hands. Distraught emotion consumed Maria as she grasped the pen. The barrier of reserve was ready to break as she signed the relinquishment as untold thousands had done before her. Maria's words faltered as she tried to provide the sister in charge with information about the child. She furnished the nun with the child's father's name, her street address, their ages, and a birth country. She proclaimed the child's name to be Sophia Kaminsky.

Broken promises rushed up to meet Maria as she stepped

inside her flat on Villa Avenue. Once inside, her heart exploded into fragments of sorrow. Holding the contents of her previously stretched belly, she rocked back and forth on bended knees upon the cold hard floor of the dank apartment, retching in grief. She reflected on the sweet face of her baby as she held a recently swaddled blanket to her cheek, drinking in the smell of creamy warm milk. Her arms would never embrace the weight of delight, soft and warm again. Maria struggled through tears, reflecting on the words Mother Jerome echoed as she reluctantly left the Foundling's building, "You must love your child very much to save her." Maria leaned on the nun's words, accepting her own broken heart in order to permit her child to live.

II

By five o'clock each morning, each of the six nursery floors of the New York Foundling Hospital was in a flurry. The Foundling, a large expanse at 175 East Sixty-Eighth Street in Manhattan, was managed by the pleated black-capped Sisters of Charity, after the order of Saint Elizabeth Ann Seton. The New York Sisters took the rule of helping the poor—from Saints Vincent de Paul and Louise de Marillac in France—and spread their work among the children at the orphanage, giving them much-needed care. Nurses and matrons were full of life everywhere, and all had four or five children with them. Baths had to be given, hair washed and combed, and teeth brushed. Hand-sewn garments lay neatly upon rows of bedded cribs ready to outfit seventy-five toddlers from two years up to age six. Earlier, Mother Jerome and Sister Teresa Vincent made an announcement in the direction of the nursing staff that another group of children would be leaving them. This was nothing new. Employees of the Foundling had prepared children in the past, often three and four times a year since 1869, and June 26, 1917 was no different.

75 Foundlings Off To Find Homes
Will Meet in West the 'Fathers' and 'Mothers'
Whom They Never Have Seen

Seventy-five eager children from the New York Foundling Hospital, accompanied by two Sisters and eight nurses started on the New York Central Railroad at 1 P.M. yesterday for homes selected for them in the West. All have been told they are going to live with their 'fathers' and 'mothers' and all are happy in the thought of seeing those persons.

Every year the New York Foundling Hospital sends 400 or more children for adoption, and yesterday's lot was a remarkably fine one. Naturally, the youngsters were greatly excited; for they were leaving the only home they had ever known and were going to those before mentioned mysterious 'mothers' and 'fathers.'

– *The New York World*
June 27, 1917

Nuns, nurses, and agents of the Foundling wiped runny noses of whimpering children at being parted from the only home and affection they had ever known. They straightened eyelet bonnets, hooked loose buttons on shiny black leather-top shoes, and tied dangling strings of laced-up boots in their line of vision. To take the children and their caregivers to Grand Central Terminal, a street car remained ready outside the Foundling building. Some of the children were so small they were carried in the arms of nurses and nuns.

Retired police officer Jan Coffrey laid his strong but gentle hands upon each head of the seventy-five as they passed by him. A hint of moisture swelled in the kind gent's eyes as he called them all by name. To some extent he considered himself a godfather to each and every child entering the Foundling Hospital's doors. Like his comrades at the precinct, who often delivered the abandoned to one of the Sisters in charge, Jan Coffrey made it his duty to know each child by name.

As each child's head was anointed with devout kisses, nurses, doctors, and nuns of the Foundling were struck with their physical weaknesses and fought off the first gathering of tears. The emotional strain would challenge the assembly often; the process of gather and release repeated itself often in the course of sixty years. Many of these children had been in the orphanage since they were merely a few hours old. They had been found with life almost extinct, in hallways, waiting rooms of subways, elevated stations, church steps, piers, ash cans, and other out-of-the-way places. Several guardians indulged in recalling past events when infants first arrived on their doorstep at 17 East Twelfth Street, followed by the brownstone at 3 North Washington Square, where a white wicker cradle stood in the foyer. Babies were often deposited with notes attached to clothing or keepsake articles placed close by, from desperate mothers asking the good sisters to care for their children. So many children arrived this way, parallel to their immigrant parents—new in America, weakened by way of religious, social, and economic well-being—leaving parent's little choice but to surrender them.

Five leather-bound albums entitled "Letters Left on Babies by Their Mothers" once placed at the New York Foundling Hospitals headquarters at Avenue of the Americas and Sixteenth Street in Manhattan, now rest in quiet slumber in a repository of the New York Historical Society. Snippets of unique sentiments remain fixed within the folds of the letters, a piece of fabric torn from a dress or a ribbon from Ulysses S. Grant's re-election campaign. These are responsive trinkets that would one day identify children so that their mothers might claim them. These letters reveal more than the adversity of surrendering a child for adoption; rather, they provide evidence that foundlings have always been born more of poverty than of neglect.

The infants name is Harry Fields, one month old. Some day I shall try to reward you, good Sisters, your laudable undertaking. I might have in a moment of desperation committed a crime, had not your door opened to receive the waif of an unfortunate erring one. Never deliver the child to anyone unless they can bring the mate of the article enclosed or produce undeniable proof that they are the genuine parents.

–Anonymous
April 28, 1871

My Dear Sisters,

I am obliged to give up my beloved son as I have no home to stay in, and he has been sick for six months, and I have two more children, and my husband is dead. When I get well I will send him some things. I hope that you will be kind to little Charles Parker. He has been christened into the Roman Catholic Church. I hope that you will excuse his dear mother for not sending his clothes clean. I have suffered for the last eight months, and now I will suffer forever more. Pity me now for my baby dear. I hope that you will let him stay with you, and not give him out. He is on the breast. May God and the Blessed Mother take care of my baby and pity me. Charles Parker----goodbye my baby!

Signed,
Mrs. A.B. Parker
June, 1872

These two dollars are to have the child baptized Willie. Do not be afraid of the sore on this face. It is only ringworm. You will remember this badge for him.

–Unsigned
1873

For the love of God, and his holy mother, will you keep the little baby who was left in the crib last night; I will give anything you require. Her father is a wicked Orangeman. I told him it was dead because I want to have her raised a Roman Catholic, and have nursed out. I will pay all the expenses.

Will you, dear Sisters, remember a kind mother's heart? If I do not see her again, I will never do any good on this earth. I work at dress making for a living. My husband gives me but a third of his earnings because I am a Roman Catholic. Be kind to my little lamb. If she should die, please bury her for me. Write to Father Farrell, Barclay Street Church, and state circumstances to him. Pray to the Blessed Virgin for me to help me through.

1875

To the Sister,

This child, one day old, and will be claimed as soon as possible, but how soon I do not know. All expenses will be paid in full. His name is Willie C. I tied a little turquoise locket around his neck, please let him wear it. Please do not have the chain and locket taken off. Let the child have it all the time so as to be identified, that no mistake be made. My poor dear daughter may come to reclaim her child in a short time, and she is so agonized for fear she may get a child not her own. I can not understand how a simple number can ever identify a child. For God's sake grant my request; you will never have to regret it.

A Mamma
January 14, 1877

Babies at the New York Foundling Hospital are marked with cards tied to the waists of their little gowns. Two babies sleep together in a crib, and when the children are undressed for the night the cards stay with the clothing worn by the child ready to be put on in the morning. When a baby is sent out to board (for wet-nursing) or wherever the child goes, the card is worn marked with all necessary information and assigned hospital number. These numbers date from the first child received, and include all of the children either born at the hospital or those taken in.

Police officers deliver abandoned infants at the
New York Foundling on East 68th and Lexington.
Courtesy of the New York Foundling

Sisters of Charity accepting infants at the orphanage.

Courtesy of the New York Foundling

III

Babies straddled hips of caregivers and nuns through the waiting room of Grand Central Terminal, while uneven crowds watched with curiosity. Eight nurses scurried to keep the regiment of children in order as the opal-faced Seth Thomas ticked perfect time prior to boarding the one o'clock *New York & Chicago Special*. Little waifs they were, the discards of New York, out in search of homes to take them away from the center of sorrows and woes they had been born into. They were bound for placement inside the far reaches of America, with mysterious mothers and fathers whom they have never seen. At the helm of the group, two Sisters of Charity walked with quick, decisive steps, indiscriminately heralding to individuals along the terminal, "These children are foundlings going to homes in the Western plains where babies are greatly longed for," and to others along the side track, "These children will breathe fresh air, and many will live on farms. Some will go to homes with wealth and culture. Imagine these children going out today will make their way in the world."

Two-year-old Sophia Kaminsky was among the seventy-five. She had been at the orphanage a year and a half, before an order came through matching her description. Much like placing an order through a mail-order catalogue, a family from Minneapolis, Minnesota had requested a girl around the age of two, with brown hair and brown eyes. Upon the application, the family noted they had three sons of their own with the same coloring, and they wanted a girl to match. Through the years, agents of the Foundling traveling at the forefront of departure addressed clergy across America of the need for family homes. In return, word passed throughout congregations and settlements, and prospective parents simply filled out an application indicating specifics wanted in a child, such as age, gender, and special features. Heritage was also matched within families, if identified.

Sophia, feeling forgotten and lost, held tight to the warm hand of one of the sisters. There was no mother or father near to reach out and quell her fears; the child was on the verge of leaving behind everything her young life had known. The child whose hand was held would vaguely remember cries and lurid color, a blur of thick curling smoke mixed with confusion, and terror not half understood. When she was very old she would wonder over the randomness of detail, for if she had not happened to be there, with the others who were of all colors, shapes, sizes, and previous conditions of servitude, her whole life would have been different. The young girl's glinting brown eyes told of daydreaming solitude, setting apart a round and pleasant olive-toned face. Too young to comprehend the gaunt spectra of an unprotected past, her chin-length orphanage bob, the shade of ancient oaks sheltering a forest pool, escaped randomly under the brim of a delicate white eyelet as her head somberly rested against the nuns spiritual black sleeve.

Sweet-faced nuns bustled about, smoothing children's homespun garments while inspecting embroidered hems and shirt collars for acceptable names and birth dates. A dozen employees arranged bows of ribbon in assorted colors stamped with prearranged numbers pinned to the clothing of each child. There could be no mistake in the role of trim color; its identification determined each child's state destination. The numbers remained vital, fating a match-up held by prospective parents awaiting arrival of a potential child at train stations in several far-off states. There was Mary, No. 9, blond and blue-eyed; Carmela, No. 29, dark as a gypsy with sloe black eyes of far off Italy; and Bayley, No. 33, of County Claire, Ireland; Edith, No. 41, with Titan curls above a face of Scandinavian ivory; Patrick, No. 30, a noisy little firecracker with hair to match, and William, No. 25, a sturdy lad who had Bill written all over him if any stocky boy ever did; Emma, No. 31, with melting brown eyes and golden hair, and Reinhardt, No. 38, with a strong German accent fixed in the midst of the assembly.

"This girl's name is Mabel Rubin, a Jewish name," exclaimed Hanna, one of the nurses examining a ripple of thread stretched along a stiff gauze scrap fixed upon the clothing edge.

"No matter, names change in new families. Every child entering the Foundling, regardless of religion, will go forth as a Catholic. None will be the wiser," replied the nun as her eyes gazed toward heaven.

"This baby has no name sewn into the hem of her dress," asked another.

"That one was delivered by one of the police officers found at the Ferry House at Greenpoint Station on the Brooklyn pier. We judged her life existence as ten days old, and call her Baby Girl. Don't worry; her new parents will give her a name. Many of the parents in the West prefer to rename their child. In any case, we just need to make sure they get a home."

"And what about this one, sister?" asked one more.

In front of them stood a three-year old wearing a long white dress. The child's apparel included a large red ribbon tied within a bulky form embellishing long pleasing curly black hair. "The name sewn on the dress hem is Gaetano. This is a boy, Sister! But he looks like a girl. A beautiful little Italian girl at that, or boy!" maintained the caregiver.

The nun waved her hand in the air as if to push away the assertion. "Never mind. The new parents who ordered him will soon discover they indeed have a boy. Fear that more girls have been previously requested to keep farm women living in desolate areas company, it was necessary to make certain we had a few boys on this trip, giving the impression of a girl if needed. Now then, where is our agent, Mr. O'Shea? It's time to get these children boarded."

Several matrons set out to pass through netting serving as a bed for babies too young to sit. The grid would serve a dual purpose, keeping out the cinders and dust aimlessly wafting through the car from the fire-box fueling steam to the locomotive. The children were going out across America in a hundred different directions as seventy-five pairs of baby eyes peered from the windows of the special drawing room car attached to the line of coaches of the New York Central. Some onlookers standing in the gloomy smoke-soaked atmosphere of the rail yard quietly wiped away silent tears as they witnessed the pathetic scene before them. Just now, in France, American troops waved their campaign hats under General Pershing, receiving welcoming cheers from crowds, as Sophia's train slowly disappeared from New York.

Children ready to board an orphan train
at New York Grand Central Terminal in 1923.
Courtesy of Al Appleton and the New York Foundling.

Tag number 33, worn by train rider,
Bayley Talty, (Reverend Albert Perrizo.)
Courtesy of Donna Brooks.

Shoes and socks worn by train rider,
Marie Roberts, (Mary Daly/Carter.)
Courtesy of Mary Cary [daughter of Marie Carter.]

Bayley and Marie rode on the same orphan train
with Sophia from New York to Chicago before the children
switched trains taking them on into Minnesota.

Coat, shoes, and tag [gauze cloth sewn into the hem of coats and dresses for identifying children coming from the New York Foundling Hospital] worn by train rider, Agnes Chambers. ("Pat" Patnode/Thiessen.)

Courtesy of the Pat Thiessen family.

IV

It took several days for Sophia to arrive in Minneapolis. *The New York & Chicago Special*, affectionately known as "the baby special," left New York City on the 26th of June carrying children and guardians along the northwest route of train No. 41 to Buffalo, New York. Twelve hours later, at 12:55 a.m., air brakes hissed as the Chicago bound train arrived at the New York Central Depot under a misty veil scaling the sky from east to west. The first leg of the journey had left everyone staggering ballet-style down the aisles due to the poor coach suspension system on the day train. The children traveled by day and evening hours; refraining from all night travel in their own car as the assembly rested along a siding shed. Measuring the number of stops ahead, agents telegraphed train stations for fresh food supplies for the children. After a brief visit in Buffalo, the children's car passed onto the connecting train of the New York Central No. 83, *The Empire Limited*, departing at 5:03 a.m. The consist of passengers, children, mail, and baggage provoked an average train speed of twenty-six miles an hour traveling beside the southern water level route of Buffalo and Niagara Falls. As the train converged where land meets water along Pennsylvania and Lake Erie the steamer rolled on toward Cleveland, Ohio. By 8:30 p.m. *The Empire Limited* pulled into Cleveland as doughboys marched toward the train station as part of the American Expeditionary Forces heading for Europe. Feeling the effects of fatigue, the children and their nurses spent the night in an unchanged routine. The following day, the children's car joined the New York Central train No. 23, *The Western Express*, departing Cleveland at 11:00 a.m. carrying the precious cargo on through Indiana and into Chicago, Illinois. Several of Sophia's train companions set out earlier in various directions. Several traveled by boat into Canada, while others were transported to new family homes at whistle stops.

The train from Cleveland, Ohio to Chicago was the slowest and therefore the cheapest train. People paid more money for tickets on faster trains, and orphanages placing children west opted for the cheapest tickets the railroads would sell them. While the railroads primary cargo was agricultural products to urban markets; the west was also short of farm labor. The railroads, particularly the western railroads, embraced the migration of children as a way to help farmers and ranchers obtain free farm labor. Indentured child labor was emphatically in the railroads self interest. The Milwaukee Road [designated rail names the Chicago, Milwaukee, St Paul & Pacific; Chicago, Milwaukee, St Paul; Chicago, Milwaukee, & Puget Sound; Milwaukee Land Company; and Milwaukee & St Paul] held an interest in the delivery of children of the orphan trains for farm and manufacturing labor. A passenger ticket office in New York City employed by the Milwaukee provided access to cheap tickets purchased by the orphanages for Sophia's train journey destined for "Milwaukee Road" country.

From Manhattan to Buffalo, to Cleveland and rolling along into Chicago, the trains carrying the cars of children traversed the southern shores of three Great Lakes--- Ontario, Erie, and Michigan. As *The Western Express* glided into the LaSalle Street Station in Chicago at 9:00 p.m. everyone felt the effects of exhaustion.

"Settle the children down," a weary nun instructed several nurses. "Tomorrow is a big day, and we must have the children in good form. As you know, Chicago [and St. Louis] is the division of rail lines taking these children further west to meet their new families."

"Do they all leave from this station?" an inexperienced nurse queried.

"Some of the children will of course, "explained the nun, "but others will need to be transported by streetcar over to Union Station to meet western trains leaving with our assistants."

Sophia departed Union Station on June 29, 1917 at 10:10 a.m. aboard train No. 17---*The Columbian* of the Milwaukee Road --- her last train home. Her indenture papers were in order. The legal agreement dispatched her under the name Sophia Kamin. Perhaps the name Kaminsky echoed German, Polish, or Ukrainian, with or without Jewish attachment, but the new name, Kamin, would give the child a new identity and a fresh start. Scores of children would come to learn later in life that indentured children who were not legally adopted were ineligible to inherit from their families unless specified accordingly in an official last will and testament. These children would learn of loving families, and of abusive ones. They would feel loved, and unloved. They would feel like members of a family, or experience forced labor imposed as punishment, or be taken by unknown parents as bonded servants.

The indenture insisted on written correspondence between the Foundling and the prospective parents every six months concerning the child's welfare. It directed parental responsibility toward clothing, education, financial stability, and treating each child as his or her own until the age of eighteen. For those children entirely satisfied in the family, foster parents might encounter a probationary period of three months to put forward a legal adoption. The agreement also specified the New York Foundling could remove a child from the family at anytime without court presence should placement proves unsatisfactory.

As the carload of chubby, dimpled little bits of humanity arrived in St Paul/ Minneapolis, Minnesota at 10:35 p.m. after traveling 1,350 miles; baggage hustlers, express men, and station attaches at the depot stopped their work to gaze in wonder at the car attached to the train. Curly heads—brunette, blond, and auburn—bobbed up and down. There was a minimum of crying and lots of laughing.

When the conductor came out of the car there was a suspicion of moisture in his eyes.

"I won't go through there again," he said. "They're happy, but it's too pitiful. They all wanted to shake hands with me, or caught hold of my hand and looked up at me and smiled as I passed. I suppose they are taught to do it. There are all kinds, and are sweet as babies. It is a shame they will never know a real mother and father."

The following morning, on June 30th, Joseph O'Shea, thin and short in stature, stepped onto the Minneapolis depot platform off the branch line of the Milwaukee Road. Little Sophia wrapped her delicate baby arms tightly around the agent's slight neck. The child's head rested timidly under a thick, worldly mustache, balancing sleek black hair. Her mint-green satin ribbon imprinted with the number seven, tagging her pinafore, rested on the visible side as the child pressed closer to the agent. In next to no time a man rushed slightly ahead of a woman, and an elderly man and three young boys trailing close behind beckoned the agent. He waved ticket number seven above his head as his free hand nervously patted a greasy and heavy cowlick positioned awkwardly atop an unruly ebony mane.

"Ah, you must be the Duda family?" Mr. O' Shea questioned as the group arrived while struggling to extend a handshake with the child in his arms.

"I'm Joseph, and this is my wife Mary and our sons, Christopher, seven; Frank, five; Joseph, three; and my wife's father, Frank Melich," Joseph Duda said, slightly out of breath. He stood gangly, with narrowing eyes the bluish-steel of a midwinter day. He motioned to each with an uneven index.

"I have a special delivery for you," the agent articulated. "This little dark-haired beauty is Sophia," he said, offering the child to Mrs. Duda as the girl gripped tighter to the agent's neck. "She is very shy, as you can see," he added, prying away the child's hold on him, "but I'm sure you will all get on just fine as time passes."

Mary Duda, a slight woman with brown hair parted down the middle and pulled tight into a bun, longed for a girl to provide with pretty, delicate dresses in exchange for companionship. The couple's sons, sturdy and vigorous, were a handful at times, and she had begged an often mulish husband to apply for a girl from the New York Foundling. A priest and family friend who married the pair years before in Gilman, Minnesota, notified the Twin Cities family of the desperation facing the children in New York, and by what method the Catholic organization farmed them out to families in the West. The priest told the couple that many children off the trains were received in the Rochester, St. Cloud, and Minneapolis and St. Paul area.

Mary fixed her deep and lustrous dark eyes, upon the child held before her. She would fit in quite agreeably, she thought, with the family's Polish-German background.

Joseph and Mary completed the usual questionnaire prior to leaving with their family in the homeward direction:

Where do you live? *4306 Penn Avenue North, Minneapolis, Minnesota, Hennepin County.* What trolley line runs closest to your home? *Chicago and Penn.* How far do you live from the nearest train station, and what line of railroad? *Five miles north of the Milwaukee and St. Paul.* Do you rent or own your home? Give a brief description. *Own a two-story frame dwelling.* How old are you? *Husband thirty-two and wife thirty.* What is your religion? *Catholic.* Where were you married and by whom? *Saints Peter and Paul Church, Gilman, Minn., Rev. Joseph A. Dudick.* Who testifies to the worthiness of your application for said child? *Rev. Joseph A. Dudick.* Who is your witness? *Frank Melich.* What is your current occupation? *Husband, a machinist helper. Wife, a homemaker.* Do you agree to write to the Foundling reporting on the child twice a year? Will you see to it that the child attends Mass and Sunday school regularly? Will you notify us of any change in address? Do you expect to adopt the child if she/he proves satisfactory? *Yes entirely.*

For the next year and a half, Sophia would not speak. Her playful spirit was broken. She would not sleep in the bed provided her and was often found curled up in a corner of the floor, fast asleep.

"Mary, we need to send her back to New York. She is a backward child, like this rag doll your father gave her. Motionless!" commanded Joseph as he tossed the doll to her.

Mary Duda loved Sophia. She wanted this little girl more than anything and thought that with a little more patience from her husband Sophia would come around, but Joseph was insistent in pushing Mary to compose a letter to the Foundling asking them to retrieve the child.

"Tell them we want to send her back. Tell them she is stubborn. Tell them we can't make anything out of her. Tell them we prefer our own children to this one," Mary's husband's voice boomed. Thus pen was put to paper.

In the course of communication, Mary dispatched three letters. Each time, the New York Sisters' written reply was the same.

"Please take into consideration the child is only three years of age. We have striven to reason with you the fact that she is still young and will come around. Emotional trauma spawned from extraordinarily stressful events may shatter a sense of safety and securities, making one feel helpless and vulnerable. Every part of this is grounds for the child's defense."

Following the final correspondence, the couple decided to give Sophia another chance. They considered shifting their family from Minneapolis to the wide expanses of the countryside from whence they had originated; Browerville and Little Elk Township in Todd County.

᪥

On September 25, 1918, Surgeon General Rupert Blue, announced to the Associated Press the first cases of influenza had been discovered in Minnesota. The number of influenza patients who needed the attention of physicians and nurses overwhelmed St. Paul and Minneapolis clinicians. The Minneapolis City Hospital and St. John's Hospital in St. Paul were solely devoted to treating influenza patients. At City Hospital, Superintendent Dr. Harry Britton reported that the "hospital was presently caring for 150 cases and had about 70 on the waiting list. Beds were available for the waiting numbers, but there were not enough healthy nurses to care for them." As in the rest of the country, Minnesota's first cases were directly traceable to soldiers, sailors, or their acquaintances. Every military base and military hospital in the Minneapolis–St. Paul area was severely affected. Case isolation was slowly implemented at both Fort Snelling and the Dunwoody Naval Detachment (military installations in Minneapolis), expanding their case loads and leading to immediate quarantine. Less than a week after the first report implicated the state health board, more than a thousand cases of the Spanish Flu were reported in Minneapolis alone.

Two major issues contributed to the gravity of the flu pandemic: the war effort and limited scientific knowledge. But, despite the lack of understanding about viruses, advice to curb infection was relatively accurate. The Minnesota State Board of Health recommended the use of handkerchiefs to cover sneezes and coughs, plenty of fresh air, avoidance of the sick and of crowds, and physician care when stricken. Minneapolis ordered 15,000 gauze masks from the Red Cross on October 1, 1918. These were used by nurses in schools and hospitals, by doctors, by hospital visitors, and by those suspected of being infected. On November 6th, government officials of St. Paul, the twin city of Minneapolis, enacted a closing order for the whole city, including schools, theaters, churches, and dance halls. St. Paul chose to utilize isolation, and Minneapolis did not. In the meanwhile, mail carriers distributed educational materials on their routes and Boy Scouts distributed posters to stores, offices, and factories in downtown Minneapolis. Minneapolis teachers who were put out of work by the closing of schools were asked to volunteer for health education campaigns.

Case reporting varied between the two cities. Individuals with influenza who had their status reported in St. Paul had to endure isolation until they were released with a physician's approval. Discouraged individuals seeking the attention of physicians, and thus being reported, brought on the undesired consequence of enforced isolation. Subsequently, to prevent homes from being quarantined, physicians were not reporting their cases, and hundreds of persons in the city did not call for medical assistance until the last minute, therefore pneumonia had already set in. Dying patients consequently struggled for air until suffocation.

At least two different vaccines were administered in Minneapolis-St. Paul. Bacteriologists at the University of Minnesota produced a serum alleging to prevent pneumonia. Mayo Clinic in Rochester,

Minnesota, churned out a vaccine intended to prevent both pneumonia and influenza. Both vaccines we ineffective; neither actually contained an influenza virus.

Disputes arose and continued throughout the pandemic. Minneapolis closed schools on two separate occasions, October 12 through November 17, and December 10 through December 29, 1918. In Minneapolis and St. Paul there was no single message to deal with issues, and fear of governing authority failed to take decisive action, ultimately leaving many individuals to make their own decisions.

Minneapolis and St. Paul
Influenza cases and deaths
September 30, 1918 to January 6, 1919

	Minneapolis	St. Paul
Total Deaths	747	645
Total Cases	14,411	4,399
Death Rate (per 100,000)	264	300
Incidence Rate	4,781	2,049
Fatality Rate (percentage)	5.2	14.7

The Spanish Influenza of 1918 to 1919 killed between 50 and 100 million people worldwide over the course of two years, making it one of the deadliest natural disasters in human history. It killed more people than the causalities of World War I. Mary Melich Duda died of the Influenza Pandemic less than twenty-four hours after admission to City Hospital in Minneapolis. Dr. Harry A. Britton declared her expired at 11:30 p.m. on December 16, 1918. She was thirty-three years old.

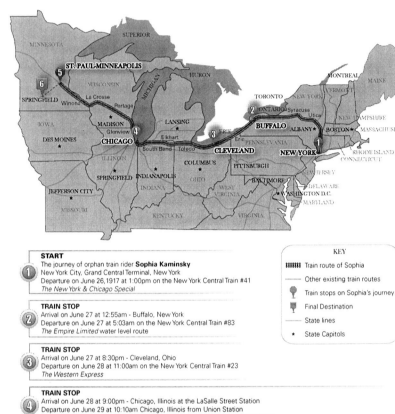

KEY

▦▦▦	Train route of Sophia
‑‑‑‑‑‑	Other existing train routes
⚱	Train stops on Sophia's journey
⚱	Final Destination
‑‑‑‑‑‑	State lines
★	State Capitols

START
The journey of orphan train rider **Sophia Kaminsky**
New York City, Grand Central Terminal, New York
Departure on June 26, 1917 at 1:00pm on the New York Central Train #41
The New York & Chicago Special

TRAIN STOP
Arrival on June 27 at 12:55am - Buffalo, New York
Departure on June 27 at 5:03am on the New York Central Train #83
The Empire Limited water level route

TRAIN STOP
Arrival on June 27 at 8:30pm - Cleveland, Ohio
Departure on June 28 at 11:00am on the New York Central Train #23
The Western Express

TRAIN STOP
Arrival on June 28 at 9:00pm - Chicago, Illinois at the LaSalle Street Station
Departure on June 29 at 10:10am Chicago, Illinois from Union Station
Chicago, Milwaukee & St. Paul Train #17 *The Columbian* of the Milwaukee Road

TRAIN STOP
Arrival on June 29 at 10:35pm - Minneapolis, Minnesota at the Chicago, Milwaukee & St. Paul Station, Minnesota
Entire journey miles: 1,350
Departure: June 30, 1917, two-year-old Sophia disembarked *The Columbian* with
prearranged indenture papers to a Minneapolis family

FINAL DESTINATION
Relocation of four-year-old Sophia on January 19, 1919 to Springfield, Minnesota
due to unsatisfactory family circumstances in Minneapolis

Sophia's Journey Map.

Courtesy Morrison-Maierle, Inc.

V

January 15, 1919

I have Mr. Hudson's letter, with sample importation blanks, and will see him tomorrow and try and arrange with him so that we will not be held up in getting the children into this state. Yesterday, I got the child Sophia Kaminsky, who had been in the Duda home of North Minneapolis, where the St. Paul Children's Protective Society interceded. I will take her over to nearby St. Joseph's German Catholic Orphanage, which is managed by the Sisters of St. Benedict in St. Paul. Sister Juliana Venne, is the superior in charge of placements, and will keep Sophia until arrangements can be made for her transportation to New York. I will continue to look for a home for the child here in Minnesota. I don't think I ought to have any trouble in placing this child again.

Edward J. O'Shea
Agent for the New York Foundling Hospital
The Hawthorne Hotel
12th Street and Hawthorne Ave.
Minneapolis, Minnesota

Born in the Češnjica village, in the province of Krain—Carniola's historical region and duchy of Austria in today's Slovenia—Francis S. Rant had studied philosophical and theological studies at the Saint Paul Seminary in Minnesota and was ordained a priest there. On January 16, 1919, the forty-four-year-old priest, pastor of St. Raphael's parish in Springfield, Minnesota, satisfied his yearly visit to St. Joseph's Orphanage while returning from a holiday trip in Germany.

Sister Juliana welcomed the visiting priest, and before long conversation turned to Sophia. "A New York Foundling Hospital agent working in this city brought an all-but-four-year-old girl to us yesterday. She goes by the name Sophia. The child was taken off an orphan train from New York by a Minneapolis family, but the foster mother had recently died of the influenza epidemic. The father, having three young sons of his own, felt he could not take on the responsibility of another child as well. He's leaving with his three sons for a farm in Swanville. Mr. O'Shea is preparing to send the child back to New York unless another family in Minnesota is found immediately."

The priest mused upon Sister Juliana's words as she went on. "We have over 800 children of our own here at this orphanage, Father. They need placing with families of German heritage, or with any luck, once on their feet they can return to their natural parents. The agent indicated this girl had origins of German from one of her natural parents, but no one had asked for her in New York. I don't think we can help her. She is New York's responsibility, but I feel the trauma of a return trip may be too much for the child. She barely speaks."

Father Rant, a supporter of the poor and suffering, proposed a plan. "I am acquainted with a childless widowed woman in my parish. Her name is Anna Greim, born in Friederichs Hutte, Germany, speaks only German and understands limited English, but I'm sure she could use the help of a girl one day. She has no living relatives and is alone, her husband Joseph now deceased. Might you search out the New York agent in favor of consent while I speak with Mrs.

Greim upon my return to Springfield?"

Sister Juliana contacted Mr. O'Shea. In return, Mr. O'Shea contacted the Foundling in New York. The Foundling, in support of reinstatement, dispatched a new indenture in favor of Sophia Kamin en route to Anna Greim, at 321 Cass Avenue North, in Springfield, Minnesota. The woman and her home would not be investigated for approved placement because a priest had put forward the prospective placement.

❧

Sophia did not have a good feeling when—on January 19, 1919—she stepped into the kitchen of the tiny four-room wood frame dwelling. Sister Raymond (Clara) Otto, a sixth-grade through eighth-grade teacher and office worker at St. Joseph's Orphanage, held her hand. In the course of the one hundred and fifty mile trip to this southern Minnesota town, the nun yielded a sermon in the direction of the young child that she would meet her mother. As a result, the girl smiled with bright eyes at the woman Sister Raymond alleged as her mama, but Mrs. Greim did not appear happy, casting her off like yesterday's dust.

Standing before the child stood a squat woman supporting her elbows and forearms across a dull, unhappy, ankle-length dress. Thin and disagreeable lips surrounded an expressionless face. Long hair streaked with gray and yellow spun a firm knot atop her head, and the woman's identity appeared antiquated beyond her fifty-three years. The nun, herself from Germany, communicated with Mrs. Greim in their native language that the New York orphanage would be in touch. Imparting a vague eye in the direction of the little girl, Sister Raymond asked Mrs. Greim if she could have a look around the premises before leaving.

Anna Greim stood silent as the nun set off, moving swiftly through the house. Her unrestricted black habit took on wings as her senses scanned essential elements. A kerosene lamp rested upon a plain wood table, telling her there was no electricity. A red hand pump stood tall amid a chipped porcelain basin, delivering water for dishes and wash cloth bathing, since there was no bathtub. A white-washed ceiling, cracked and flaking, loomed over a cook stove fueled by wood stacked neatly in a nearby box. A pantry supplied dishes, pans, and home preserves consisting for the most part of sauerkraut and lard. The adjoining two rooms, a bedroom and living room, were closed off by windowless French doors occupied by a rent-paying couple scarcely home. An outhouse in the back yard served as a toilet for all. The house, with stingy little windows, appeared as stripped as the expression on the child's face now seated near the warmth of the stove. As she walked outside into a shroud of blue dusk, Sister Raymond could only pray the priest had known what he was doing by proposing this home.

"*Ins Bett,*" she said, pointing to a single, brown wrought-iron bed filling space in the center of the bedroom. A three-drawer dresser existed under a single sepia photograph of Anna and her late husband, Joseph Greim. A Standard treadle sewing machine occupied the balance of the floor, as Anna, extinguishing the hurricane lamp fire, repeated, "*Ins Bett.*" Climbing into bed with the old woman, Sophia felt tears in her eyes. She was in terror that they might fall, one slow, piteous drop after the other, forcing her to flee from the room and later face questions. In her customary Germanic nature, Anna reached under her pillow for a rosary and began praying. The child remained quiet, her thoughts clutching ambivalent fears, as guttural Teutonic hisses escaped the stoic woman's lips.

From the start, nearly every resident of Springfield became the little girl's surrogate mother and father. Because no orphan trains arrived in Springfield, Sophia became somewhat of a novelty among their citizens. Parishioners of all denominations embraced the orphan girl with open arms. But Anna Greim saw neither the uniqueness nor the unparallel joy a child could bring. Instead she disregarded the girl of no use until the age of eight, at which time Anna put a new meaning to the phrase, "all work and no play," or retribution would surely follow.

Sophia went to school, and in the sphere of idleness took on scrubbing floors, washing dishes, dusting, and babysitting at the homes of doctors, lawyers, and bankers. The affluent citizens of Springfield recognized the young girl needed more help than the old woman provided. They offered assistance of clothing, aside from the dowdy flour sack dresses Anna provided. They encouraged meals taken with their families, and from time to time the young girl would slip flavorsome provisions into her pocket to enjoy later. The habit would remain with her a lifetime, for mealtime at Anna's consisted largely of lard bread and potatoes and noodles drenched in lard. Meat was a rarity, and when available, Anna meant for it to last weeks beyond its natural shelf life.

Although the well heeled provided the little village girl with strong and positive emotions of regard and affection, in no way did the girl ever take delivery of a hug or kiss from the woman she called mother. Christmas would never exist—outside of attending church—with so much as a gift or greeting from Anna. The girl would recall in later years one occasion she had been handed an orange on Christmas Day. She had never tasted an orange before and remembered the wonderful citrus blend of sweet and tangy juice spraying delight across her taste buds.

Aside from worshipping God on Sundays and praying her

nightly beads, the most important mission in Anna Greim's life was to keep her indentured servant working hard at all times. The local bank president and his wife set aside two dollars a week intended for the girl's necessities in exchange for her work. The money aided the girl by means of a toothbrush, eye glasses, dental work, and her own personal bed. Funds provided well-being of health for a tonsillectomy recommended by the school nurse, confirming that the girl had the worst diseased tonsils ever seen in the entire history of the school, due to Mrs. Greim's failed attempt at swabbing the girl's throat with a feather dipped in peroxide. In summer months the child was never with shoes, and in the winter she was made to wear undersized footwear, preparing her feet for future abnormalities. In the course of five consecutive years since the girl's arrival at the Greim home, a local social worker documented that Sophia enjoyed a favorable home and was bright and happy.

⁂

In exchange for chopped wood, Anna took in laundry from a bachelor living across the street from her home. Sophia carried large, heavy pieces of split wood to and from the basement, keeping the wood box by the cook stove filled at all times. Sophia managed the old crank washing machine that hummed a rhythmic chug as it rocked in place along aged planks upon a back porch. She made beds, scrubbed floors, dusted, and domesticated inside and outside the home while achieving schoolwork and learning the English language under the dim of a kerosene lamp.

In straw hat weather an unparalleled fear met the girl. Divided sections of potato and cabbage plants occupied Anna Greim's backyard garden. Cabbage was an important staple for Mrs. Greim; she preserved numerous jars of sauerkraut. Potatoes by the gunny sack found a home inside the root cellar. On this particular day, Anna instructed the child to harvest heaps of potato bugs sprinkled about the many potato plants, then let the insects fall inside a container of kerosene, *"in der karosene."* After that, the cabbage worms.

"Please, no, I don't like it," the now ten-year old balked with distaste.

"Deutsch sprechen zu mir, (Speak German to me)."

The young girl quaked in error hearing the petulance in Anna's voice.

"Ich habe Angst, (I'm afraid)."

Anna commanded the girl to do as told, or *"Ich sende Ihnen mit den Zigeunern.* (I send you with the gypsies.)" The young girl had no idea of the meaning, but Anna gave the impression it was something bad.

Through all of time, potato bugs have been the world's most universally feared, hated, and disgusting creatures. Slightly ahead, Sophia saw the striped backs of many as they crawled slowly along the plant leaves, their legs working stiffly and jerkily. The girl rebelled, standing her ground and refusing to touch the insects and creepy-crawlies. She soon found herself positioned over a backless chair placed inside the corner kitchen.

"Bücken Sie sich, (Bend over)," Anna demanded.

Anna reached into the shadows of the corner for a plaited black-snake cane. With a steady hand and practiced eye she raised the instrument of torture. Like a hungry hawk on an innocent chicken, intense force delivered several violently swift blows that descended upon the girl's quivering flesh. Sophia closed her lips firmly so that not even a groan might escape. She did not scream, for she was too proud to let her tormentor know what she was suffering. She braced herself mentally and prevented the chastisement from breaking her spirit. Anna advised the girl to remember to do as told next time or after that, *"nisht goot,* (not good)."

As soon as she was released, great welts swelled with pain and bruising. The malady of blackened upper legs, which she had to keep out of sight, would occur repeatedly throughout the youth's life. Whenever Anna considered the girl to have misbehaved, she imposed ill treatment. With no protection, the girl believed she was unable to give testimony to anyone against Mrs. Greim and feared she must have deserved punishment for having done something wrong.

VI

About the time Sophia reached the age of fourteen, Anna Greim was of the opinion that the girl needed no further education. She thought of school as foolishness. A similarly outlandish and cruel thought prevented fresh air from entering into the youth's bedroom, now the attic. During hot summer months Anna nailed the one small lonely window shut, disallowing ventilation.

Contempt burned in Sophia when she discovered school excluded from her days. She thought back to an earlier time when she had worked hard in school to learn the English language, especially during her formative years, when she had had no choice but to learn German at home. However, she had made worthy friends, Dorothy Solentjes and Helen Lang, who lived within walking distance of her house. The threesome often had walked to and from school together. The day Sophia told her friends she was not permitted to finish her freshman year of high school, the duo informed her that Anna Greim was not her real mother.

"Sophia, you're a real chum. You know Dorothy and I love you like a sister, and we'd never say or do anything to hurt you, but don't you know Mrs. Greim isn't your real ma?" questioned Helen. "My ma says it's so, but never to talk about it. Everyone in town knows it. The fact is—the whole town has been trying to raise you right behind Mrs. Greim's back. We all love you."

"You're pretty, Sophia. You don't look anything like that ole bat," Dorothy chimed in.

But Sophia laughed nervously. She thought, "*Is this true? If Anna Greim isn't my real mother, than who is?*" She was aware of the distance of affection Anna gave, not like other children's parents expressing love with soft kisses and warm embraces, care she had never received. She felt that perhaps Anna was unfamiliar with child-rearing because she had no children of her own to practice unbending behavior or that perhaps the woman's sour mind had been influenced by fending for herself as a young, penniless widow. Perhaps she was simply hard hearted. Sophia's friends informed her that Joe Greim was a gentle voice, but Anna never spoke of him.

Yet, in spite of everything, the people of Springfield loved her. The man across the street from her home selling eggs and milk always greeted her with a warm and friendly, "Hello, Sophia, how's my favorite girl today?" Mr. Stieler, at the bakery, offered her day-old confections that were as excellent as fresh. The town doctor often declared when seeing her, "Stop by to see me anytime you feel sick, Sophia, no cost." Often the girl wanted to tell the doctor when the back of her legs hurt from Anna's floggings, but she knew that fearful words from a child's lips held no influence with an adult and were better when kept silent. Pastor von Fischer invited Sophia often to come into his church anytime she needed to talk to God. Sophia liked the pastor as much as she loved the people of the town. Other children's mothers would hug her, and their fathers would pat the top of her head gently. Folks praised her when she did a good job cleaning and thanked her for babysitting their children. Father Rant stopped by the house, taking in Sunday dinners now and then with Anna, but he never questioned the old woman about why Sophia was never invited to join them at the table.

At all times, the girl kept a positive attitude, but worried how she might approach Anna about having learned she was not her real parent, without getting the tar beat out of her.

Sophia didn't understand the impact of her friend's words until a week later, when she found a piece of paper in a table drawer. Her thoughts moved gingerly, like fingers not quite daring to touch. She wasn't looking for anything in particular the day Anna disappeared across the street to gather laundry from the bachelor, but barely believed what her eyes examined. Scrolled in neat penmanship, the paper revealed Sophia Kaminsky, sent west as Sophia Kamin, had been born in Bronx, New York on the 22nd day of April, 1915, and that her mother's name was Maria and her father's William. In the midst of nervous impatience, she placed the paper back into the drawer, exactly as arranged before contact. She thought the name Maria the most beautiful in the world, and then curious questions began to haunt her mind. Were her parents alive, were they dead, why didn't they keep her, where were they, did she look like her father or her mother, what did they look like, did she have any brothers or sisters? She fantasized about her mother as the beautiful, compassionate woman and her father as gentle and handsome. When nights came hard and went slowly, she pulled out magical dreams of her parents. She'd imagine herself snug upon her mother's lap, her hair smelling of bread, and feeling safe and warm. Her mother would stroke her hair, smoothing away sadness until she fell into a peaceful sleep. Her father would protect her from unhappiness and believe in her. This secret was one she favored saving from her keeper.

✻

On a weekly basis, Father Rant dined with several families in the town. At the moment, his craving for Chicken *Spaetzle* soup was set upon the home of Bill and Anne Ochs. Bill, one of three sons of Adolph Casimir Ochs, who founded the A. C. O. Brick and Tile

Company, worked the beehive kilns that produced construction brick from unique glacial deposits of high-quality clay found near a sharp bend in the Cottonwood River. The commercial product spread far and wide, and every brick building became a branded example. The priest, considering repair of the parsonage, thought to speak of the proposal at dinner as he waited for the Ochs family to join him.

In the kitchen, out of earshot of the priest, Bill quickly gathered his brood of seven, where Anne, a keenly perceptive woman, was preparing a large kettle of the soup. "I'm aware that the priest slurps his soup at full volume when he eats." At this they all chortled. "Every time he is here enjoying his broth, explosive laughter erupts from you boys, and giggling trebles from you girls," he said as he eyeballed each one of his children, aged four through sixteen. "There will be no embarrassment at the table today. I have a plan to hide your outbursts in a polite way. At the first inkling of a loud sucking noise, I'll tell a joke, in that way we can all laugh, and our guest won't know the difference. Now let's go and have some of that good soup your ma made."

The plan worked beautifully. All the more so, the priest laughed besides. Afterward, when the last mouthful of the soup had disappeared, the cleric became serious-minded. He talked of jobs drying up with the onset of the Depression. He informed Bill of the proposed renovation project, but that he needed contributions and volunteers for the development to take shape. After that, the priest turned the topic to his own accountability. "Are you aware of the orphan girl taken in by Mrs. Greim?" he coyly questioned. "I have found a small number of jobs for her with the influential of Springfield, and all have enlightened me to how partial they have become of the girl. Recently, I was informed that Mrs. Fennern has taken leave of domestic duties here. I'm curious if you've found a replacement?" tested the priest.

"I haven't come across anyone yet," Mrs. Ochs responded, "But I have heard gossip in social circles that the girl should never have been given to Mrs. Greim. My Christian presence restrains me, but I must say that the woman is as stale as last week's bread."

Bill cleared his throat and raised his knowing broomstick eyebrows at his wife before she could utter another word. "I believe, Father, the girl has a job here."

Sophia prized working for the Ochs family. Every day was filled with love and laughter. The young boys pulled at her apron strings, and the older ones told her humorous stories, goading her into uncontainable laughter. The girls looked to Sophia as a big sister. Anne Ochs, always the mother hen gathering her chicks close, enjoyed lovingly teaching and nurturing the timid girl. Sophia found happy contentment under the shelter of Anne's wings, and the woman took great pleasure in her wise and protective role. "You can talk to us about anything, Sophia," Anne proclaimed. "We don't shove anything under the carpet here." Despite walking the mile-long train track twice a week, Anna Greim on no account allowed Sophia's presence at her new employer during her leisure time.

※

The youth was coming of age in a repressive household, drawing comparisons, and regularly felt much like Cinderella. With the wood reclaimed to a polished luster, the girl was always hard at it scrubbing worn floor boards with lye soap made from ashes and the lard Anna rendered. While taking up needlepoint, the fleshy old woman settled herself into a pint-sized blue rocker as she watched the girl clean. A knock at the front porch door stunned the old woman as she glimpsed through the thin cotton corner hanging nearby.

In no way did Anna Greim write the Foundling in the eleven years since she had received Sophia at age four. A social worker of Minnesota's Child Welfare Board made known in her latest assessment that the Greim home was unfavorable. This was unlike an earlier assessment from another. In describing Sophia's foster mother, the employee had determined, "She is a very strict, mean, and miserly woman, almost to a fault." The worker recommended removal of the girl from the home, writing, "Sophia has grown tall and very thin, and is forbidden recreation and school." The county worker transmitted the aforementioned conclusions to the Minnesota Board of Control; early investigative responsibility in Minneapolis fell briefly upon the organization. The Board outlined letters to the New York Foundling, acknowledging "a great disservice has been done to this girl by placing her with an elderly woman with no interest in her welfare, who works her hard, and by no means allows the girl recreation." The Foundling, realizing trouble with one of their children, promptly dispatched Miss Marie Geraghty, their own private social worker, to investigate.

"*Gehen Sie Zimmer. Halten Sie ruhig.* (Go to room. Hold quietly)," Anna nervously commanded, waving arthritic fingers at the girl as two women stood past the window in formfitting silhouettes of synthetic textile and cloche hats.

Upset, Sophia ran up the five steps to her undersized attic room and shut the weakened, skeletal door against strong German words. If walls had tongues, those that enclosed these cells could tell of the girl's fear. She was unsure if she had done anything wrong, but wondered who was at the door, the police? Silently, giving attention to the squeak of the tension spring drawn tight against the moss-green screen door opening and slamming shut several times, an inquisitive mind drew her to a break in the door. She heard subdued conversations of two women's voices. One woman's voice had a strange yet familiar accent, making the girl feel strangely comfortable.

Tensions ran high as the group carried on a debate of adoption and home removal. The screen door banged with a vengeance as Anna Greim made her way ahead two blocks to the home of the local bank president, where Sophia had previously worked. The spring groaned again as Miss Geraghty arrived where Anna stood rapidly speaking German to the banker's wife, asking for rescue. Within minutes, the threesome returned to the Greim home, with the banker's wife as interpreter. The New York agent implored the local bank president's wife to look after Sophia for the next three years, she'd be eighteen before long, out on her own, and making her way in the world.

The banker's wife argued she had two daughters of her own to look after, and another was impossible. She conveyed the aid she and her husband had already facilitated toward the girl.

Mrs. Greim rebelled in German that she was lonely and needed the girl to care for her.

Meanwhile the county worker drew Sophia into the picture, appealing for her participation. "Let's hear what Sophia has to say about all this," she prevailed.

As the teen entered the room of adult women, she had a painfully growing need to confide in someone. Only this minute, as the girl was on the verge of executing pent-up emotion, the New York woman spoke up, affecting the familiar tone of voice.

"Hello, Sophia, my name is Marie Geraghty. It is so nice to finally meet you. I have a message for you from the Sisters in New York. They wish for me to send you their love. And police officer..." Sophia froze at hearing the word "police." If her suspicions were true, they were coming to get her. Miss Geraghty went on, "..Coffrey especially wants me to fill him in about how you are. He knew you when you were a mere baby."

Sophia was stunned. A hazy reflection entered the girl's mind of train whistles, children, and pleated black bonnets held by far-reaching grosgrain around sweet-faced nuns. "Are you happy living here, Sophia?"

To some extent, Sophia's self-reservation remained guesswork, obstructing the girl's clarity of mind. She became apprehensive of dispatch back to her forgotten New York, perhaps to be placed in an orphanage. She feared the vivid beatings dished out by Anna if she told of ill treatment. Instead, the girl shed tears, her lips unmoving, and rushed back to the security of her room. As a result, the parody continued on without her.

The unfurling of the girl's self-possession shared gentle emergence and the dramatic breaking of shells. Everyone seemed to have a plan for her. Miss Geraghty put forward a plan of adoption. The girl would gain social prominence in the community and grow to be an heir someday to the elderly woman's estate. Mrs. Greim alleged in German she possessed a will, and held that the homestead one day would belong to Sophie, as Mrs. Greim called her. The girl would have an inheritance, but only if Sophie remained with her always. The county worker asked Mrs. Greim if she indeed had a last will and testament. Perjuring herself, Mrs. Greim acknowledged, omitting Sophie from her will, but she would have the paperwork changed. The banker's wife felt strongly that Mrs. Greim should adopt Sophia to obtain her estate upon death. The New York worker again projected approval of a legal adoption. The idea flew like a lead balloon with the county worker. The county worker recommended questioning individuals of the town about the suitability of the girl's present home.

The inquiry began immediately. The county operative went about in a methodic, unhurried way, initiating several door knocks at past and present employers of the girl. Each brought forth diverse consideration. The banker was of the opinion Mrs. Greim did not own much property and that there would be nothing left for the girl. Father Rant thought it unwise to take Sophia out of the home at this time, and recommended adoption. The local doctor and a nearby pastor favored Sophia remaining in Mrs. Greim's home only if advantageous to the girl, but at this point, given that she would reach the age of eighteen in a few years, they felt the girl's benefits rather useless. The county worker discussed her study report with the local attorney, and he estimated the Greim estate was worth two thousand dollars. He was concerned that Anna Greim would need all the property she now had to see herself through. The county worker felt the property clause should not be an inducement for a contemplated adoption, and pointed out that if the adoption was to be, a new last will and testament ought to be drawn in favor of Sophia and filed with the County Probate Court, rather than left at a bank to be changed at any trifling provocation.

The lawyer sent a letter to the State Board of Control asking for direction in this matter. The reply specified, "We believe cases of this type, where a child has been so completely removed from her own relatives and has lived in a strange home so long, a legal adoption should be promoted for reasons of legal standing in the home." By society's standards, the county worker thought bleakly of the legality of such an idea because Anna Greim's persona remained strict, brutal, and insensitive. The worker feared the girl's days would dwindle away to complete darkness.

VII

The town's scheme for Anna Greim to adopt Sophia was thwarted. One excuse after the next was used by Anna as refusal of an agreement. Either she couldn't manage a convenient time to leave Springfield for the County Courthouse thirty miles away, or she was frequently ill, or lacked transportation, even though inhabitants of the town volunteered the undertaking. For two years the citizens of Springfield persisted in moving forward an adoption for Sophia, with the intention of securing a future inheritance for the girl, in spite of Mrs. Greim's deficiency in love and affection.

When Sophia turned sixteen, letters of persuasion on behalf of Mrs. Greim, written by Sophia, went forth to the county worker, to the State Board of Control, and to the New York Foundling, expressing a non-adoption. Mrs. Greim didn't want Sophia as a legal daughter, and Sophia was sure she didn't want Mrs. Greim for a legal mother. The New York Foundling and the State Board of Control soon made contact with each other.

The New York Foundling Hospital wrote the following:

> We have considered the matter very carefully and concluded there is no use in trying to force Sophia and Mrs. Greim to complete an adoption, because the girl and her foster mother have decided against it. Sophia's standing in the home and community is just the same as before. If we agree with them to put off an adoption, maybe we can induce Mrs. Greim to treat Sophia more reasonably. In the

event the Greim home becomes unbearable for the girl, and should any future dissatisfaction occur and Sophia wish to leave, do you think the banker and his wife, who have befriended the girl in the past, would assume responsibility for her? This would not be as severe a rupture to Sophia as a plan to bring her back to New York.

The Board responded as follows:

Please work out a plan for closer supervision of the girl with your agent when she is in this state. We have received firsthand information from the community at large that Sophia is having a difficult time and that Mrs. Greim forbids the girl further education. All the more, the girl wishes to go to dances and would enjoy some recreation time, but Mrs. Greim is in bed by 7:30 p.m. and expects the same of Sophia. The girl has no time for entertainment after work hours. We feel a grave injustice has been done this girl in that she was placed with an elderly woman who is unable to efficiently care for her. We hope your agency will do all that it can to readjust the situation.

❦

Dorothy and Helen rushed to meet Sophia as she walked home from work at the Ochs'. Helen, an irrepressible chatterbox, talked of the dance that night at the Patterson Ballroom, "You just have to come! There's a traveling band in town performing tonight, and tomorrow is the big Sauerkraut Day Celebration. Isn't it exciting?"

Dorothy's father was the leader of the Sauerkraut Band, an ensemble playing the town's homeland German music. A Sauerkraut Queen would be chosen and carried in her gilded carriage along the Main Street storefronts. Sitting beside her, duty bound, would be the Sauerkraut King, determined by his ability to eat the most sauerkraut. A procession of parade floats, doll buggies, bands, horse-drawn wagons, tricycles, and bicycles would subsequently follow the honored couple. Stands sprinkled along Main Street would dole out enough kraut and beer to fest goers, making full bellies made of steel and weak stomachs ill.

"It's been a year since social workers have tried to argue some leisure time, but Anna still doesn't allow me out at night. Besides, I have nothing to wear," the cheerless girl replied.

"We thought about that for you," Dorothy said, eagerly holding before her friend a paper-wrapped parcel. The girl quickly unfurled the package, presenting a simple yet feminine outfit of navy blue cardigan, a white blouse, and a button-down wrap skirt, the hem line somewhere between the knees and the shin. Sophia knew she had the best friends in the world and hugged each of them. Then she stepped into the fading afternoon sun toward home. The girl held an idea, as if in the palms of her hand.

Sophia professed fatigue as Anna went to bed at her usual time. Within the half hour, the girl tip-toed to the side window along the front porch, glided the frame, and moved quietly through the opening. She was taking an awful risk. Quickly running down the road, she looked east toward home. She felt she ought to return, but there was a need to experience going to a dance and being with friends.

The dance turned out to be everything she had hoped. She loved dancing. She twirled, wiggled, and swayed with Dorothy and Helen to sweet champagne music. And she met Charlie, a farm boy from a nearby town, well-mannered, confident, dark and handsome. He asked her for a dance, and she shyly accepted. Later, he joined the table of friends and showed Sophia what a fun guy he was to be around. "I'm pressing charges against you," Charlie said looking directly at Sophia, "for stealing my heart." Sophia blushed then he enlightened her with funny stories, making her laugh. They talked of the latest bank robbery over in Okebena, fifty miles away, and "Did you hear the Barrow gang got away with twenty-five hundred dollars and dodged every bullet as they ran from Okebena's First State Bank? That Bonnie Parker must be something to put up with the likes of Clyde Barrow," Helen said. "I just want a good man to settle down with someday. Have lots of kids, and make them a good home. You know, love 'em to death and spoil 'em rotten."

At this they all laughed, except Sophia. Dorothy noticed. "Sophia, Helen meant nothing toward you. What you have to go through living with her. My mean list would fill a catalog."

Charlie looked at Sophia perplexed, and she soon opened her heart. She told Charlie of the actions and events of her young life, of the unjust oppression Anna Greim had inflicted upon her, but Charlie had reservations. He couldn't believe anyone could be treated that harshly until Dorothy and Helen reinforced Sophia's statements.

"Everyone in town knows how that old witch treats her, but no one can do anything about it. In a year her indenture is finished, and she is free," Helen bantered.

"You're a slave?" Charlie asked in the direction of Sophia.

"I guess I am, but only to Anna. The orphanage in New York City, where I come from, does not intend for the indentured agreement with Mrs. Greim to be carried out this way. The Sisters in New York saved my life, and for that I am grateful. They want loving families for all their children, but sometimes it doesn't work out. They know of trouble with Mrs. Greim because many social workers have been to the house. They just don't know how much trouble. I'm afraid of being sent back to New York, among strangers. I'm not familiar with any relatives. I've been in this town from the time I can remember, and I have my best chums and people in town who love me. I can live on that," the girl confessed.

"This is absurd," commanded Charlie. "You're coming home with me. My folks aren't rich, but we have a house full of kids and plenty of love."

Sophia could have stared into Charlie's bright sea-blue eyes all night long, making her heart melt. With her fingertips she felt where the wound had knitted together so long ago, on her leg. It felt like Braille only she could decipher, communicating cruelty and pain and making her realize she needed to get home. She wasn't supposed to be gone in the first place, and at a dance of all places.

"I must go. It's nearly eleven o'clock, and if my step-mother finds I'm gone, I don't know what might happen," she said, departing.

But Charlie was right behind her, offering her a ride home in his folks' Model T Ford Runabout. She asked him to drop her off one block short of her house. Charlie hesitated leaving her go. He wondered if he'd ever see her again, because he seldom was able to leave the farm and his father's sawmill business. He nervously waited until he was sure she was safely inside the house. From his distance he could see her by the illumination of the street lamp, but she had not gone inside.

Sophia moved quietly, paying close attention, and cautiously slid the window she had escaped from earlier, but it wouldn't shift. She tried again, at which time the window flew up with a bang and the black snake whip beat time against the sill.

"*Schlafen auf der Veranda wie ein Hund* (Sleep on the porch like a dog)," the old woman commanded in a sharp tongue.

"Certainly you can't make her sleep outside, here, in the cold," the voice of Charlie now spoke from the side of the open porch. He had followed feeling compelled to make sure she was safe.

"*Gehen Sie, oder ich rufe die Polizei für das Nehmen eines*

Minderjährigen ohne Erlaubnis zusammen (Go, or I summon the police together for taking a person under age without permission)."

Charlie knew German, for it was his social background. He pleaded with the old woman to let Sophia inside, and Anna agreed, but only when convinced the girl's suitor was gone. Sophia told Charlie to go. She'd be alright. She didn't want her step-mother damaging this boy's warm, affectionate heart and sterling qualities, and Charlie reluctantly left.

That entire night, Sophia felt the chill of the cold porch floor seeping up through her feet, overshadowing her essence.

＊

On the eve of the Great Depression, the orphan trains ran no more. Mrs. Greim prevailed upon Sophia to write another letter to the Foundling Hospital. The girl's irredeemable behavior of attending a dance had been intolerable. The orphanage dispatched two letters.

> Our Dear Sophia,
>
> We understand that you attended one dance, which offended Mrs. Greim, and for that reason, Mrs. Greim does not wish to adopt. Sophia, we do not wish to take you back to New York, as long as your report continues as good as at present, and will not think of doing so. However there are advantages that would come to you from an adoption, and we believe you should have them. It will be well for you to consider the advantages of security and inheritance. Might you consider an adoption at this time?
>
> Mrs. Greim, it appears that you do not understand the advantages of legal adoption for you and Sophia. You have had her in your home since 1919 and have enjoyed having her and learned to depend on her. She has been a good and faithful companion to you, and has given to you as your

own daughter a youthful society you very much needed. You should give her the confidence and assurance that comes from feeling that people really care for one another. This feeling of security is given to the girl by legalizing her and giving her the rights to your name, and at best your heritage. Sophia is entitled to enjoy the normal pleasures suited to her age with supervision and protection. There should be some arrangement made allowing her some recreation. You know that all work and no play make Jack a dull boy. I am sure you will be glad to cooperate with Sophia and allow her leisure time in a normal way becoming to girls of her age and station in life. The local banker of your town has told our agent Miss Geraghty that he would be glad to take you and Sophia to your local courthouse anytime you want to complete the adoption. We believe it is your duty to do this for Sophia, and we will be glad to hear that you have given her this well-earned station in life.

That year, Sophia cautiously looked for her freedom. She became proficient inventing harmless lies, disappearing to buy needed postage stamps, or declaring work when there was none. Other times she'd leave for Helen or Dorothy's house, when instead she'd meet her friends to window shop along Main Street. The country was already feeling the onset of the Great Depression, with unemployment and low levels of trade and investment leaving little money for Sophia to set aside to buy herself things. On this particular day, her seventeenth birthday, Sophia found an opened letter placed upon the table when she returned home.

April 22, 1932

Sophia Dearest,

Do you miss me anything as much as I miss you? Can we meet again at next week's dance? I hope that you are getting on well, with no further setbacks with your step-mother. She is an angry crusader to say the least.

I have nothing so interesting to tell in the way of news. I am working with an expert in avian veterinary medicine in poultry diseases, with many tests to render. Everyone calls me Doc, and I enjoy working with our feathered friends.

I am sorry I find little time to write. My folks keep me and my brothers busy. This past week we dug a half mile ditch with hand shovels, just for water run-off.

If there is anything I can do for you, just tip me the word. I look forward to seeing you. This is an invitation and a promise.

Love, Charlie

Sophia met Charlie at the dance, and the pair bargained for many more fun times together. The extra work imposed upon the girl by Anna, and the many nights spent on the porch floor had been well worth it to see Charlie. Nearing seventy, Anna was slowing down, and the whip was no longer used, but the old woman's verbal abuse was equivalent. *"Stoppen Sie, diesen Jungen zu sehen, oder zurück zu New York gehen Sie* (Stop seeing this boy, or you go back to New York.)"

The citizens of Springfield made a last ditch effort, pushing Anna Greim toward formalizing a legal adoption for Sophia. Wanting to keep the girl for reasons of work and sought after attention in old age, Anna conceded. The village attorney drew up the legal papers, and Mrs. Greim scratched out her name on the documents in halfhearted penmanship. The attorney drove Sophia to the county courthouse, and on May 18, 1932, seventeen-year-old Sophia was legally adopted as Sophia Greim. Anna Greim marked the occasion of legalized motherhood by refusing to attend the adoption, and remained at home.

VIII

Snowflakes danced in on a frigid Canadian cold front that froze most of Minnesota as Sophia sat in the kitchen at the Ochs. She warmed her hands around the cup of tea and drank as Bill, Anne, and Vincent, one of their sons home on visit from St. Paul, posed an employment opportunity.

"There's a family in St. Paul, Walter and Mary Villaume, who need help. I've known the Villaume's for a time, and they're looking for an employee to serve their meals. You wouldn't have to clean or cook or take care of their two boys, Walter Jr. and Eugene." Vincent laughed at this point. "I have no idea why, but the boys are called Tug, and Weisser. Funny pet names if you ask me. In any case, the parents both work out of the home. Walter is the president of the Minnesota Macaroni Manufacturing Company, where *Jenny Lee* macaroni is produced, and his wife is a nurse. If you take the job, Sophia, you can live-in with this family."

Anne poured Sophia another cup of tea. Round and round went the pretty spoon, and now she paused, studied the teaspoon, and thought about the proposal. The job would take her far enough away from Anna Greim, but she'd miss Charlie and her friends. She felt the need to go away for a while, to venture off further than the confines of Springfield. But then contemplating the thought suddenly gave her giddy enthusiasm.

"I'll take it," she announced as a final decision, "but what do I tell my, my mother?" she questioned with difficulty in uttering the word "mother." She used the term only when necessary for reference; she still thought of her as foster mother.

"Now don't worry your pretty little head over Mrs. Greim. Bill and I will take care of everything. Vincent can drive you to St. Paul, and we'll tell Mrs. Greim the job pays much more than any job you could ever obtain around here. You can send half of your earnings to her, but it's entirely up to you, Sophia, how much you want to send. She will never know how much you are making, but supplementing her income may be very persuasive.

⁂

It was twilight when she arrived, and sections of smoke loomed from above, balancing the glow of large windows shining like burnished swords engraved within an impressive two story brick house, the color of reddish brown. Sophia stood in the walkway, clutching her small cardboard suitcase containing few possessions. The house, she thought, was every bit as grand as Bill and Anne's. She wondered if it was made of Ochs brick. The residence ranked in line with similar homes along Portland Avenue, in the neighborhood of Lexington. Lighted pillars glowing like jewels welcomed a well-lit carriage house. She wondered if it might be the servant's quarters where she'd live. Sophia approached and rang the bell. A maid answered, "Can I help you?"

"I'm Sophia, here for the server's job," she shyly replied.

Mrs. Villaume immediately came to the door. She was a blond, petite woman of German lineage, a model of refined simplicity, wearing her nurse's uniform, softly shaped with easy, graceful lines embellishing a coveted badge of service upon her apron. "Regretfully, I've not had time to change my wear, but do come in, my dear. Vincent has told us so much about you." Mrs. Villaume proceeded to give Sophia a tour of the five- bedroom and three-bathroom house while telling the girl of her duties. "You will be expected to help the maids with cooking or caring for our sons in your idle hours, but foremost our evening meals are to be served on time. We entertain guests quite often here, and it's important everyone is well cared for."

The rest of the maids living within the city came in by day, and soon Sophia met Esther, a girl from Iowa with a Swedish nationality, and Myrtle from Wisconsin. One day while on break behind the house, Esther offered Sophia a cigarette. Having never tried tobacco, Sophia was hesitant, but Esther told her, "You haven't lived until you've smoked." Sophia attempted to inhale the smoky flavors of the lit tobacco, then coughed and nearly choked, deciding against further offers of the vice.

When the pair returned to the kitchen, Myrtle was busy preparing food. "Sophia, can you lend a hand?" Myrtle implored. "Take these fish out back to the butcher block and clean them." Not to appear imprudent, Sophia obliged, carrying four large walleye in a pan. She had never cleaned a fish in her entire life because this food staple had never appeared on the plates at the Greim home. Seating herself upon a stool, the girl thought, *"How do I go about peeling off the skin, what about the guts?"* She had cleaned chickens before, so she thought cleaning a fish must be handled in the same manner. Sophia went back inside the house to ask for help, but Myrtle and Esther were nowhere in sight. The girl boiled a kettle of hot water and carried its contents outside. Taking fish in hand she dropped them into the bubbling water in one piece, waited a minute, and then withdrew the lot with tongs, laying them upon the block. The fish appeared shriveled. When cool enough to handle, she removed fish heads, tails, skin, bones, and edges of meat that had started to cook. It worked like a charm, and Sophia felt confident she could handle the job again if requested. Esther rushed around the living room with dust feather and cleaner in hand in a tizzy when Sophia entered, carrying the cleaned fish. "Mrs. Villaume just called, and we are to prepare a banquet for the *Jenny Lee* board members gathering here tonight. The lady of the house wants her angel skin dress pressed then laid out on her bed. Would you be a sweet, Sophia, and do it?"

"What is angel skin?" Sophia questioned. "The pink one," Esther stated as she moved off to clean the next room.

Sophia found the dress in her employer's bedroom closet. The Villaume's home boasted electricity, and Sophia found the iron. She had never used an electric iron before. She was use to the forged flat irons she'd heat on the stove. Then testing the iron with sprits of spit, making sure it sizzled, she knew the iron was hot enough to smooth out wrinkled clothing. But she wasn't sure how to test one running on electricity. The Greim home still did not have the luxury of electricity. Sophia moved the iron switch ahead, but failed to tap the base with her fingers, testing the heat. The beautiful angel skin dress arranged neatly upon the iron board was now branded with a perfectly stamped image of the iron. Sophia didn't know what do but cry. Myrtle and Esther came running when they heard the girl's sobs. Their eye's registered disbelief when they caught sight of the burnt trademark. Then the pair burst into laughter.

That night, after the dinner guests were served and fed, Mrs. Villaume, wearing a navy chenille suit, sought out Sophia in the confines of her bedroom. She comforted the girl, telling her not to feel bad about burning her dress. "It could happen to anyone. Besides, I was thinking of giving that old rag to the Salvation Army anyway," she said, pinching her lips into the shape of a suppressed smile. Sophia considered that had the calamity happened at Mrs. Greim's, the result would surely have incurred punishment.

July 6, 1934

Dear Bill, Anne, and Ochs Family,

The Villaume's are very nice to me. Mr. Villaume is French, but I'm perpetually serving more plates of Italian spaghetti and pasta goulash. I do all the washing, ironing and cooking. The children, one-year-old Tug, and three-year-old Weisser, are the responsibility of another maid. Though full of energy, I've already taken to the boys. You know how I love children, which prompts me, "Please give little Bootsie [a pet name for the Ochs' son, Norbert] a hug and kiss from me."

I am not sure if "big city life" is for me. It feels very strange, but I'm sure in time, I will get use to it. Please write and tell me all the news.

Lovingly,

Sophie, (or as your kids call me, "Fosie")

July 11, 1934

Dearest Sophie,

We were all glad to get your letter, and to note that you are pleased with your work. That's the stuff! Keep up the good work!

The whole gang here was fighting for the chance to read your letter. You wouldn't believe how many people here in Springfield have read your letters. Everyone wants to know how you are!

Oh yes, and your good friend, Charles, stopped to see us recently. I promised not to mention this in my letter, but I don't expect he'd mind that we did not live up to the promise.

Just remember to be careful, and be a good girl, as we have told you before.

As Ever,

The Ochs Gang

Within a few short months of working for the Villaume's, a telegram arrived for her.

September 18, 1934

Come home. Your mother is sick.
You must quit your job.

Charlie

"That's strange," she thought as she read the Western Union message, *"Charlie is sending the telegram? This must be serious."*

As ever the obedient daughter, Sophia left St. Paul immediately in the direction of Springfield. Once home, she found Anna Greim was no sicker than average. Instead it was Charlie who missed her, and Sophia was annoyed at his trickery, making her come home under false pretenses. But when Charlie showed up at her door the next day, her heart raced for him, her breathing quickened, and her muscles tightened. The significance of him became clear to her. Without need for proof or evidence, she felt an unshakable belief in something. Pulling her into his arms, Charlie whispered seriously, "Will you marry me?"

IX

In June of 1936 Sophia met Charles at the altar. Before the couple's commitment of love before God and man, the officiating priest baptized her because he was unsure if the girl had been baptized before boarding an orphan train in New York. Mrs. Greim had never bothered to have her indentured daughter baptized, so the religious rite was required before a marriage could take place. Few wedding invitations were sent out because Anna Greim refused to assist with cost, but the church was filled to capacity. Nearly every resident of Springfield attended the ceremony to see "their daughter" married. Sophia couldn't have been happier. Later, a spectacular wedding reception was held at the home of Charlie's parents.

Anna disliked Charlie, even though he was intelligent and articulate, but she was never quite ready to set Sophia free. Her subservient daughter and new husband lived with her in the tiny little house on Cass Avenue. The couple faithfully accommodated Anna's every need. Charlie found work in the trade he knew best, as an avian veterinarian doctor. When the couple's first two children were born in the little house, Anna was surprisingly elated. As the two girls grew, Anna used them as pawns to antagonize Sophia further. One day, while luring the girl's into her bedroom, Anna tempted, "*Kuss Oma. Kommen Sie, ich habe Hänsel und Gretel, Ihnen zu zeigen.* (Kiss grandma. Come, I have Hansel and Gretel to show you)." Sophia had never glimpsed the statues herself as a child, and proceeded to follow her daughters to the bedroom. Once they reached

Anna, she slammed the door in Sophia's face and locked it, saying, "*Sie bleibt aus.* (She stays out). "

The girls each held Hansel and Gretel, examining the painted bisque children in delight. But as if God works miracles in small ways in giving or taking away, the girl's both dropped the baked-clay figurines. The statues broke into a million little pieces, reduced to a pile of ruble on the hardwood floor beneath them.

৵

Anna Greim died in 1954. She was eighty-five years old. Sophia attended her funeral and burial, but never once returned to Anna Greim's gravesite. The three grand essentials to happiness in life are something to do, something to love, and something to hope for. Sophia found all three in raising her family of five with her prince charming, finally finding a family.

After marriage, Sophia was required by the Social Security Administration to search out her certificate of birth. A birth record identifies who you are, represents your family, and gives you the ties that bind. There is power in a name, but one or several character changes can link you to everyone, or to no one. You may drift through life unknowingly as to your true identity, never sure where you belong, and the foundations of generational families disappear.

New York State came up empty in locating a record. This prompted Sophia to write a letter to the New York Foundling, and before long she received a generic certificate of baptism. A Dominican priest from *St. Vincent Ferrer* performed an initiation before Sophia boarded an orphan train west, but Sophia questioned her lack of verification, "*Was I born in Europe before my parents came to the United States, and later leaving me at the orphanage? Was I born in another US state? Did my birth go unreported? Did the orphanage*

implicate, to some degree, identifying information in record books?"
When asked by individuals for documentation of a birth certificate,
Sophia lightheartedly responded, "I don't have a birth certificate,
but I'm here!" The baptismal certificate would serve as her identity
in this world.

> "Thus I began my new life with a new name and every-
> thing new about me. Now that the state of doubt was over,
> I felt, for many days, like one in a dream. The remembrance
> of my old life is full of so much want of hope, if it lasted
> for a year, or more, I do not know. I only know that it was,
> and ceased to be, and that I am, and there I leave it."
>
> ~ Charles Dickens

In 1960, while reading *Cedric Adams In This Corner* column
in the *Minneapolis Star*, Sophia learned of other orphans like herself
boarding trains in New York to find homes in the West. She was
stunned! All this time, she thought she was the only one. She read
on inspired. On Septemeber 28, 1958, *CBS* television station broad-
casted a five minute segment of the New York Foundling Hospital's
transfer of hundreds of children from their orphanage at 175 East
68th and Lexington Avenue to a new facility at 1175 Third Avenue.
Three women--- Carmella (Caputo) Keaveny, Marie (McGoldrick)
Lenzmeier, and Mary (Scholastica Scholl) Buscher--- happened to
watch the program, each knowing they were placed out by the New
York Foundling on an orphan train. Each questioned, *"how many
more are there like us in this world?"* In time, the women elected to
place public notice's in several newspapers throughout the Midwest
inviting others like themselves to a meeting. Nine individuals arrived in Minnesota to become acquainted and exchange life stories.

The group was unanimous in establishing successive meetings.

Letters began to arrive from nearly every state in the United States expressing a connection to life as a foundling from New York in search of forming an extended family with others like themselves. And so the meetings continued, attendance grew, and a familiar family unit took shape yearly. Sophia attended fifty of fifty-four consecutive gatherings feeling blessed to have acquired a new family ---her orphan train family. At one get-together, her biggest highlight came when she met Mary (Sullivan) Allendorf, Marie (Roberts) Carter, and Bayley Talty (Fr. Albert Perrizo) --- individuals she made an epic journey with as children on the same orphan train.

Sophia lived a full and productive life, surrounded by people she loved and who loved her. As of this writing [2013] Sophia is ninety-eight years old and remains independent in her own home. She is one of few (less than fifty) surviving children of the orphan trains existing throughout the United States today.

Sophia Kaminsky, age eight.
One of only two personal photographs as a child.

ABOUT THE AUTHOR

Minnesota author, Renée Wendinger, is a history essayist. She has received numerous awards for her work, including the NIEA award in books demonstrating excellence in history for her published nonfiction, *Extra! Extra! The Orphan Trains and Newsboys of New York*. Renée has been interviewed for magazines (*People* and the *Oprah Magazine*) and featured in countless newspapers including *USA Today*. Levels of academics have incorporated her work into learning and production.

Also by
Renée Wendinger

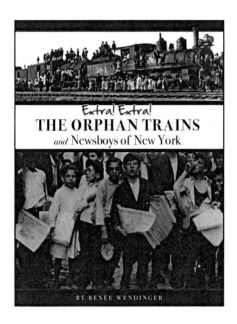

NONFICTION

Extra! Extra! The Orphan Trains
and Newsboys of New York

www.theorphantrain.com